Advance praise for *Confessions of an ADDiva*

"Learning more about ADD in women is a serious undertaking that Ms. Roggli makes downright enjoyable! Her *Confessions* while self-effacing and humorous are packed with information that offers a deeper understanding of what it's like to be a woman living with ADD. While I'm definitely recommending 'Confessions of an ADDiva' to all of my ADD sisters, in reality, it's a must-read book for everyone -- men and women alike!"

—*Patricia O. Quinn, MD, Director and Co-founder, The National Center for Girls and Women with ADHD, Washington, DC*

"A page turner! Captivating! Validating! Honest and humorous! This is *not* your typical book on "coming to terms with ADHD. Linda quickly earns the title of 'soul sister' by candidly and unabashedly opening her heart to her readers. She invites us into the most painful and the most joyful moments of her life. In her unique 'ADDiva-ish' way, she is able to describe our deepest doubts and fears. And as we journey with her, she instills hope and courage to finally step out, live a life of possibility with AD/HD and, most importantly *be yourself!*"

—*Nancy Ratey, Ed. M., MCC, SCAC, author of* The Disorganized Mind: Coaching Your ADD Brain to Take Control of your Time, Tasks and Talents

"Linda Roggli has been there and is now telling the tales! She has incredible heart in recounting the struggles, but such infectious enthusiasm that you'll love laughing and crying along with her. You'll also wonder if she has been spying on your life. This may be the first book that you actually finish and then you'll be sorry to see it end. Linda will be your new best friend and confidante. After the first chapter you'll know why she is one of my favorite people!"

—*Ari Tuckman, Psy. D., author of* More Attention, Less Deficit: Success Strategies for Adults with AD/HD

Advance praise for *Confessions of an ADDiva*

"*Confessions of an ADDiva* offers much more than a mirror in which to recognize yourself or, if angled slightly, someone you love. In *Confessions*, Ms. Roggli invites you to step around the mirror and consider a world where the gifts of your energy, creativity and passion are embraced. *Confessions of an ADDiva* is a must-read for anyone who wants to see beyond the challenges of ADHD to the gifts that make the journey in that non-linear world worthwhile."

—*Tracy Ware, MD, Chapel Hill Psychiatric Associates*

"*Confessions* is the most heartfelt book on the experience of a woman with ADD you will ever read. From confusion to awareness to embracing the 'ADDiva' within, it is bound to inspire midlife ADD women to thrive no matter the challenges they face."

—*Judith Kolberg, co-author,* ADD-Friendly Ways to Organize Your Life
www.squallpress.net

Confessions of an ADDiva

MIDLIFE IN THE NON-LINEAR LANE

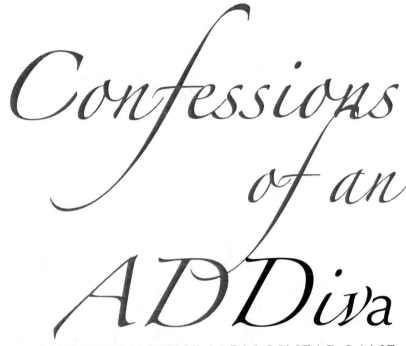

Viva! ADDiva!

LINDA ROGGLI

Published by Passionate Possibility Press
Cover design by Linda Roggli
Illustration by Wendy Sefcik

Library of Congress Cataloging-in-Publication data available on request

ISBN-13 978-0-9786409-0-3
ISBN-10 0-9786409-0-X

contents

Why are you trying to fit in
when you were born to stand out?

adapted from What a Girl Wants, *2003*

Preface

There are a lot of books about Attention Deficit Hyperactivity Disorder out there. Some of them explain brain function (and dysfunction). Some of them tell you how to change your AD/HD. Some of them offer tips and tricks to handle your AD/HD.

This is not one of those books.

This is a no-holds-barred, brutally honest account of what it's like to live with undiagnosed AD/HD for more than forty years and the startling changes that occurred after I discovered that I was an adult with AD/HD.

From diagnosis to denial, from rebellion to acceptance, I'll share my journey in a series of ADD-ish vignettes that illustrate the dramatic impact of AD/HD in my life. I'll also share my celebration of that giddy, goofy, exuberant woman who has learned to soar—my inner ADDiva!

Though I'm not Catholic, in a real sense, this book is my confessional. I am opening the door to my deepest secrets, darkest regrets, and most closeted embarrassments. After years of barring the door for fear that others would judge me harshly for my innocent transgressions, there is relief in sharing these snapshots of my life.

But this book was not conceived or written merely to air my dirty laundry. I'm deliberately showing my petticoat in the hope that other women will recognize themselves on these pages and take heart that they aren't alone. Life with AD/HD can be a challenge, but when you believe that you're the only one who misses the previews and the first five minutes of every movie you see—or that you alone can't settle down to "just do it" until the deadline approaches and the pressure's on—it can be far, far more devastating.

There are hundreds, thousands of us out here, each making our own ADD-ish way. We simply need to connect with each other, support each other, and laugh with each other. Laugh a lot. Because we reflect to each other the finest that lives inside us. We reflect to each other our hearts and souls.

This is my story. Since you're reading this book, chances are good it mirrors your story, too. If you resonate with my "True

ADD Confessions," I am thrilled. But I warn you: some of these words are not easy to hear. They may cut close to the bone of your own life or that of your sister or mother or best friend.

So read with a generous heart and an open mind, then be gentle with yourself as you allow the messages to sink in. After all, you're a bona fide ADDiva, and that's a pretty darned nice title to claim!

1

Apology kudzu

I've stopped apologizing to doorknobs. And cocktail tables. And desk corners and open drawers.

I still bump into them, of course. My brain so frequently changes direction that my body can't keep up, so I end up walking into walls or tripping on rugs.

I have an impressive and ever-changing collection of bruises on my shins, thighs, arms, and derriere. Sometimes they crop up in places I've never had bruises before. I don't know how—or when—I got them. But at least I don't say "Excuse me" to inanimate objects anymore.

You see, I found out I have ADD. That's Attention Deficit Disorder. The latest official name includes the word "Hyperactive." That makes it AD/HD, but I prefer ADD; it's shorter and easier to say.

Apparently, ADD was with me from the very beginning, but no one noticed until I was forty-five. That meant four decades of idiosyncrasies like color-coded folders and clocks set ten minutes fast. I didn't realize I was coping with a disorder that actually had a name!

Discovering ADD was the ultimate "ah-ha!" moment for me. I finally understood why I love anything that is new and interesting (it keeps my brain focused). And why I bought a hot air balloon immediately after my second balloon ride (impulsivity R me). And why, more often than I like to admit, I am late to appointments, dinners, and movies (distractibility R me, too).

My ADD brain dances to a different drummer. While the rest of the audience pays rapt attention during a piano concert, my brain is a) wondering if the velvet curtains have chains in the bottom for weight; b) noticing that my thumbnail needs filing; c) trying to remember where I parked; d) wishing the guy in the next row would stop whispering; e) worrying about whether my puppy will have an accident before I get home; f) making a list of the things I need to do at work Monday; and g) oh, yeah, catching snippets of the concert. All that in just one moment! In the next moment, a brand new set of thoughts will pirouette through my brain.

This spaghetti plate of thoughts doesn't harm anyone when I'm sitting in a concert or working alone at the computer. But add another sentient being to the mix and my distracted mind can unintentionally inflict pain.

I've blurted out an unvarnished truth during casual conversation and damaged a friendship. I've body slammed a co-worker when I was racing to a meeting, late again. I've kept my husband waiting at far too many restaurants while I finished "one more thing" at the office. I've forgotten birthdays, crunched fenders, and stepped on toes, always without malice and certainly without aforethought.

So I apologize. Profusely. Sincerely. Repeatedly.
Repeatedly.
Did I mention repeatedly?

My life has been a series of steps, missteps, and apologies. Forward march. Stumble. Back up. Apologize. I hate apologies. So I tried to fit in, avoid mistakes, make outlines, be precise and predictable. And sometimes, I could actually do it. At the outset, I could meet the deadline, stay on track, and follow the conversation. Inevitably, though, I'd sabotage my best efforts. And then apologize.

After decades of one mishap after another, I programmed the phrases "I'm sorry" and "Excuse me" on permanent speed dial in my brain. Then, when I was in the general vicinity of an accident or a problem, I'd queue up an apology—just in case.

The apology habit spread like kudzu; before long, I was taking responsibility for other people's mistakes. Then I started apologizing to dogs and cats. It wasn't much of a leap to beg forgiveness from trees and clothes hampers.

Once during my days as a newspaper reporter, when I was on my way to the typesetting office—totally absorbed in proofreading the story I had written—I ran straight into a steel pole planted in the middle of the hallway (an awkward remnant of a remodeling job). As my forehead bounced off the cold metal, I instantly said "I'm sorry"—as if the pole had every right to be there, while I did not.

Things took a turn for the absurd when I started therapy with yet another psychologist. I usually arrived late, rushing into the office with hair and coat flying, brimming with guilt (always a productive start to a counseling session). After several weeks, the therapist mentioned an interesting pattern. "Do you realize the first thing you say in every session is 'I'm sorry?'" she

Regular kudzu grows 12 inches a day.
Apology kudzu grows even faster!

asked. Without a moment's hesitation, I answered, "Oh, I'm so sorry!" I actually *apologized* for apologizing!

Something shifted inside me that day. Secretly, I was tired of apologizing for myself; being "wrong" all the time had shredded my self-esteem. I made a decision to be more selective about my humble, hat-in-hand apologies.

It took an extraordinary amount of energy and concentration (especially for a woman with undiagnosed ADD), but I forced myself to hold back automatic apologies. I bit my tongue almost to the point of bleeding. But that was just the first step.

Next, I needed to minimize my perpetual screw-ups, which would, in turn, reduce the need for apologies. I excused myself from committees because I couldn't trust myself to follow through on my promises. I reluctantly avoided starting new projects because the old ones weren't done. I refused lunch dates for fear that I would be tardy.

To a limited extent, the strategy worked. Fewer screw-ups did mean fewer apologies. But I had forced myself into an uncomfortable straightjacket, sacrificing my true nature at the altar of "Normal." And my self-esteem was still in the basement.

For decades, I had sought relief from my clenched-fist, self-loathing attitude through therapy and counseling. A succession of psychological professionals had convinced me that there was something seriously wrong with me. In somber tones, they'd tossed out a variety of unfriendly, psychological labels: "controlling," "passive-aggressive," "depressed." Now that my apology experiment had failed, I worried that I had a character flaw so daunting it couldn't be untangled by even the finest therapists or best self-help books.

The fog lifts

After my ADD diagnosis, however, the psychological fog began to lift. My psychological diagnoses could be traced back not to a troubled childhood, but to a brain that had some problems with attention and focus.

I discovered that my need for control stemmed from the chaos in my ADD brain. I felt so out of control on the inside that I compensated by controlling as much as possible on the outside. It's much like a mother who feels a draft and assumes her toddler must be cold, so she dresses her in a warm sweater. When my mind reeled with ideas and distractions, I was convinced the rest of the world was also in disarray, so I tried to impose order on it. I'll admit, it looked a lot like being "controlling."

When I was late to lunch with my husband, I wasn't being passive-aggressive, punishing him for an unidentified sin. It, too, was all about my ADD; one of the beacons for diagnosing ADD is consistent miscalculation of time. I ran late, and it was my brain that made me do it!

There is no question that I was depressed, given the problems ADD had caused in my life. Many women are diagnosed with depression long before their ADD comes to light. I found out that most folks with ADD have at least one additional psychological diagnosis (they call it co-morbidity–yuck!), so I was in good company.

Even my apology habit made perfect sense in light of the diagnosis. We ADD folks are at the mercy of our brilliant, untamed brains. While our thoughts ricochet from subject to subject, our bodies bump into furniture, spill red wine on white carpet, burn the roast, and shatter the teacup. It's a perfect storm for apology.

We shatter the teacup, then apologize

The solution to my ADD screw-ups and subsequent apologies was not to tighten the screws on my self-control or willpower. I needed to *fix* my ADD.

With zest that only an ADD brain can muster, I dove into ADD books, took ADD medications, worked with an ADD coach, went to an ADD support group, hired a professional organizer, set up an online calendar, listened to meditation CDs, labeled my sock drawer, set multiple timers, and more and more and more. Some of those things helped. Some didn't.

Labeling the sox, er ... socks drawer

After months of soul-searching, I came to a jarring realization: ADD is a lifetime arrangement. It's not going away, no matter how carefully I plan my time or organize my glove compartment. It's with me 24/7, 365 days a year, with an extra bonus day on Leap Year.

So if ADD couldn't be "cured," it made no sense to treat it as an evil invader to be vanquished. I needed to link arms with my ADD and zigzag down the Yellow Brick Road with it. In other words, I needed to claim my own ADD. I started by taking a long look back at my life.

With the overlay of ADD, previously shameful incidents took on new meaning. Instead of blaming myself for every transgression, I was now aware of the penetrating influence of ADD on my childhood, my marriage, my career, and even my happiness. I'm a bit sad that I treated myself so harshly in those early, unenlightened days. I try to forgive myself, reframing those painful memories as my best attempts to cope with powerful and undiagnosed ADD.

Living the ADD life

I'd love to report that since my ADD epiphany, I have become a model citizen: always punctual, socially appropriate, and focused. Uh, it doesn't work that way. At the most inopportune moments, my ADD brain crashes through my carefully-erected structures and strategies, bounding into the room like an exuberant puppy. And like a puppy, ADD can be adorable, unpredictable, and potentially destructive.

ADD is an eager puppy!

Yes, there are still screw-ups. I am still late sometimes (OK, I'm late most of the time!). And yes, I still apologize. ADD, after all, does not let me off the hook for irresponsible behavior or hurtful remarks. The difference is that I am not clenching my fists to prevent an upheaval nor biting back a dozen "I'm sorrys." Now, when a brouhaha occurs, I pause, breathe, and assess the situation. Then I take responsibility for my part in the situation and move on.

I still have regrets that my ADD was uncovered so late in life. For those of us diagnosed at age forty, fifty, sixty, and beyond, there is an unsettling sense that we have been cheated— robbed of youthful opportunities and starry-eyed dreams. Now that we can put a name to our wild brains, we fret that it may be too late to make up for lost time. But my experience is that there is plenty of time for us—time to forgive ourselves, time to embrace our gifts, and time to live the deeply satisfying lives we have always deserved.

The first step is awareness and understanding. In the early days of my ADD diagnosis, I desperately craved the company of other women like me who had experienced ADD from the inside out. I wanted them to share their ADD experiences with me, to tell me how they felt when they overdrew their checking accounts or spoke too loudly or apologized too often.

I discovered that most people don't talk about ADD because they don't know much about it. They have some misguided notions about ADD, as I once did: that it is strictly a children's issue; that it should be corrected through better parenting or discipline; or that it's a lame excuse for poor behavior.

That environment was not a safe place to be "out" with my ADD, so I kept it hidden (as much as I could hide something that was slathered all over my life). I smiled on the outside and cringed inwardly when people joked about "Attention Deficit Disaster" or "Always Dramatic Decisions."

But I never gave up hope that there could be a place where we could "talk amongst ourselves," share our ADD-ish stories, and serve as witnesses for each other as we moved from self-hatred to self-acceptance and self-love. In a blinding stroke of genius (and with all modesty aside), I finally established a network for women with ADD. In the process, I met dozens of women who struggled with the same sticky ADD problems I had experienced.

The network now shares information about ADD with thousands of women. Some of us are undiagnosed, perhaps blaming stress or the "change of life" for our missing car keys or confused memories. Many of us are still apologizing to doorknobs, unaware that being "different" does not equate to being "wrong."

It's time to stop apologizing for being who we are

The truth is that we are not "wrong." We are absolutely "right" and perfect, exactly as we are, despite a world that tells us day and night that we must twist ourselves into pretzels to survive in a linear society.

When we stand together, we women of ADD, we destroy the critical voices that have too long presided over our actions. We share our "ah-ha!" moments of living with ADD, those breathtaking awakenings that offer opportunities for growth. We can let down our guard and be truly who we are, in all of our wacky, whimsical glory.

I truly believe that, when ADD women fully embrace their own power, we can change the world. We simply need permission to do so; permission from each other, permission from our families and loved ones, permission from our employers and co-workers. Most of all, we need permission from ourselves to step into the fullness of our lives.

It all starts with prying open that creaky, stubborn ADD door and inviting in a little sunshine. It starts right now.

We women of ADD deserve to dance in the sunshine.

2

This is my brain on ADD

A t this point, I've stopped taking offense when someone tells me "I just love your energy!" or "I just love the way your brain works!" or my favorite, "You talk faster than I can listen!" Now I shrug and laugh with them. It would be rude to say "Thank you," considering that they're unwittingly commenting on my ADD.

Undoubtedly it was my rapid-fire conversation that tipped off our couples therapist to my ADD in the first place. And it started with my high-octane brain.

As far back as I can remember, my brain has been stuck in the "ON" position. It whirs with planning, analyzing, organizing, rehearsing, creating, worrying, thinking, inventing, learning, dreaming, and criticizing (a double dose of that one!). Not surprisingly, what bounces through my head often comes right out of my mouth in similarly wild patterns.

In psychology circles, I am known as an "External Processor." I sift through the mundane and the profound aspects of my life by speaking the words out loud. With so much going on in my head, I sometimes have a hard time deciding what gets out the door first. And time is of the essence; if my fleeting thoughts aren't released quickly, they may vanish into a black hole, never to be heard from again.

When I see a counselor or therapist, I am acutely aware that I have only fifty minutes in which to squeeze a week's worth of memories, angst, joy, and questions. So I talk even a little faster than usual. That was certainly the case when I visited the therapist who was working with my husband Victor and me on some difficult marital issues. I was seeing the therapist solo that particular week, dealing with a "me only" snag in our relationship.

Even after a long day at work, my brain was engaged and lively. I told the therapist about the latest developments in my life and in our marriage. He responded with his usual good humor. Then he asked the question that would forever alter the path of my life: "Has anyone ever told you that you might have ADD?"

I giggled; this therapist was a great kidder. But he wasn't laughing. I was confused. ADD wasn't for adults; it was for little boys who couldn't sit still in class, or who daydreamed during tests. I was too old, too female, and too focused to have ADD! The therapist noticed my dismay and backtracked a bit.

"Stop by a bookstore sometime in the next week and pick up the book *Driven to Distraction,*" he said soothingly. "Don't buy it. Just flip through it to see if anything resonates." I smiled in agreement as the session ended and somehow I managed a civil goodbye.

But as I stepped into the sharp November air, an icy half-moon glaring through a tumble of black clouds, I knew I'd never make it home without stopping at a bookstore. I needed to prove this guy wrong. Either he was crazy—or I was.

Driven to a bookstore

By the time I flung open the brass and oak doors of the nearest Barnes and Noble, I had worked myself into a state of defiance. I marched right up to the Information Desk. *(Where do you find a book about ADD—the children's section? Abnormal psychology?)* The slower-than-molasses clerk helped other customers as I impatiently drummed my fingers on the counter. Finally, it was my turn.

"*Driven to Distraction*?" he asked pleasantly. "Oh yes, that's by Hallowell and Ratey. It's in the Self-Help section. I'll show you." Dutifully, I followed him to the back of the store, although his guidance was completely unnecessary. I was intimately familiar with the Self-Help section; I'd spent many hours (and a lot more money) searching for The Self-Help Book that would fix me. I'd never found it, and I had no illusions that this book would fill the void, either.

I was mildly surprised that I didn't recognize the red-and-blue paperback he pointed out. I thought I'd skimmed through every self-help book on the shelves. But then, since I didn't have ADD, why would I waste time on a book that would merely gather dust? I grabbed *Driven to Distraction* and looked for a place to sit.

The store was busy, a pre-Thanksgiving Day rush, so all the comfortable, upholstered chairs were taken. I managed to find a vacant spot on the polished oak benches next to the magazines. I didn't bother taking off my heavy wool coat; this would take only a couple of minutes.

I glanced at the Table of Contents and then skipped through the book, reading a few sentences here and there. Nothing caught my attention until I hit Page 73 and a list of ADD symptoms:

- *a sense of underachievement regardless of how much one has accomplished*

- *difficulty getting organized*

- *chronic procrastination or getting started*

- *many projects going simultaneously and trouble with follow-through*

My mouth went dry; someone had read my diary and published it! I'm pretty sure I knocked down people in the store as I dashed to the checkout counter to pay for the book that would shake my world.

I read snippets of the book by the amber sodium vapor lights of the parking lot. Then I sneaked peeks at every stoplight on the drive home. The book stayed with me for two solid days; I read and wept, read and laughed, read with shock and understanding.

I'd found it: the reason behind my unpredictable behavior. After searching all these years, This Was It. And it even had its own catchy acronym: A-D-D. What a relief! I decided the therapist wasn't crazy after all. He was brilliant!

I read under the parking lot lights

The next morning, however, I panicked. This was a permanent condition for which there was no apparent cure. Maybe this wasn't such good news after all. Maybe I *was* crazy! Or not. As I looked again at the full list of those ADD symptoms, I began to wonder if it fit me at all.

In *Driven to Distraction*, Drs. Ned Hallowell and John Ratey offered many examples of ADD adults who had trouble getting through school, who had lost jobs and were underemployed, who depended on drugs and alcohol to self-medicate their ADD. Most engaged in high risk behaviors like skydiving or driving race cars to snap their brains to attention.

I was different: I'd done well in high school, graduated from college, and managed my own advertising agency. I'd been fired from a job only once (one of my most shameful secrets) and I rarely drank alcohol. I wasn't much of a risk-taker—no bungee jumping in my past or in the foreseeable future.

None of the other therapists I'd seen had hinted that I might have an ADD brain. I needed a second opinion.

A river called Denial

The psychiatrist who specialized in adult ADD told me to come by at 3:00 p.m. I arrived at 3:14 p.m. He wasn't surprised.

I expected a test of some kind. Instead, the doctor asked calm, one-sentence questions. I answered in rapid-fire paragraphs that jumped from one topic to another and then yet another. I talked and talked, venting my frustration, trying to explain away my mild idiosyncrasies.

As our session wound down, the room quieted and I hesitantly asked The Burning Question: "Well, uh, do you think I have it?"

"Oh, yes," he replied quickly, with what was almost certainly a smug smile.

"Really? Are you sure?" I asked.

"Oh yes," he repeated with a bigger smile. "Let's start you on some stimulant medication ..."

That was the last thing I heard. Thirty-six minutes after I'd arrived, I was back on the road to my office, a prescription in my purse and the first grenades of war exploding in my head.

I don't want to have ADD. Doesn't that mean I have brain damage? I can't have brain damage. I own my own company! I have awards on my walls! My book is in the Library of Congress!

Besides, I'm not so sure I have it anyway. All this guy did was talk to me. Maybe he misinterpreted what I said. I had a migraine, so maybe I didn't hear the questions correctly. Or I talked too fast. Or too much. I should probably call him back and apologize. Then he'll see that it's not ADD. It's just me. That's how I talk. Fast.

But what if I do have ADD? Am I stuck taking pills the rest of my life? They sound dangerous—a controlled substance. What if I get hooked on them and turn into an addict who needs a fix every day? What if the pills destroy my creativity? I have to be creative! That's what I do for a living!

OK, but if I do have it, maybe taking pills would help me get things done. I have so many things half-finished. Or maybe I could be on time. I lost thirteen minutes back in 1971 and never found them again. I'm always thirteen minutes late. Unless I'm fourteen or fifteen minutes late.

Or maybe I would actually be successful at some-thing—my definition of success. Other people think I'm already successful, but they don't know I'm fak-ing it most of the time. I feel like a fraud, afraid that people will find out the truth about me. Thank good-ness, they usually don't.

All right, if I do have ADD, what's the big deal? I've done pretty well for myself. I'm married with two kids, a career, and a nice house. I've been able to live with ADD—if that's what it is—my whole life, right? So I don't need medication or any other treatment.

I'm fine, I tell you. JUST FINE!

The internal argument went on for years, like pulling petals off a daisy: "I do have ADD. I don't have ADD. I do have ADD. I don't have ADD."

ADD clues you won't find in the DSM-IV*

- *Illegible handwriting*
- *"I have to do it my way"*
- *Profound sense of failure*
- *Feeling like a fraud; hiding yourself*
- *Overcontrolling of self, others, events*
- *Interrupting yourself*
- *Easily frustrated; quick trigger to anger*
- *Very emotional; highest highs, lowest lows*
- *Obsessive tidiness*
- *Constantly reorganizing, creating a new "system"*
- *Making simple tasks complex*
- *Inability to stick with a diet, exercise; weight issues*
- *Many intimate partners; impromptu sex*
- *Difficulty with spatial tasks–puzzles, etc.*
- *A constant sense of being "swamped"*
- *Anxiety; a baseline of unease in the world*
- *Sensitive to labels in clothes, bright light, loud noises*

*Diagnostic and Statistical Manual of Mental Disorders IV

I did try medication—several of them, in fact. Some of them made me sleepy, which piqued my interest. If my brain slowed down on stimulants, maybe it did have some wiring problems. Ultimately, medications didn't work for me (in part because I couldn't remember to take them). So I gave up on treatment.

That session with the psychiatrist did change me, though. Over a span of five years, I closed my company and retrained for a career that was far more ADD-friendly—life coaching—and eventually, coaching ADD women.

The more I learned about ADD, the more convinced I became that the good doctor (and the brilliant therapist before him) had been right about my diagnosis. Sure, I'd earned a bachelor's degree, but it had taken ten years and three colleges to do so. Yes, I was married, but it was my second husband and third marriage. (I married Number One twice!) And what passed for success from the outside certainly didn't feel like success on the inside. But did that add up to ADD? I still had nagging doubts.

Three's a charm

In perfect symmetry, it was Dr. Hallowell again who settled the issue for me. At the end of a keynote address to a national adult ADD organization, he mentioned that he was opening a satellite ADD clinic in San Diego. That's where my oldest son lived! I immediately made an appointment; finally I would take a *real* ADD test and find out from the *real* experts whether I had ADD.

The "real test" was a series of psychological evaluations. They were administered one at a time by a psychologist in a small, quiet room. There were no pictures, no noises, and no distractions. It's a perfect environment for high achievement. But these ideal conditions can actually mask ADD traits. Almost everyone with ADD performs better with no distractions, so the results of testing can skew too high. The staff at the clinic warned me not to prep for the tests by taking medications, getting a good night's sleep, etc.

Not to worry; I couldn't have envisioned a worse state of mind for my tests. I had broken my toe and was limping painfully in one of those ugly, blue, orthopedic boots. I'd had laser surgery on my face and my eyes were nearly swollen shut (my doctor had assured me that the swelling would be gone by the time I went to California). I had stayed up packing the previous night, so I'd had virtually no sleep.

I got lost on the way to the clinic, my cell phone was dead, I wound up in rush-hour traffic on the busiest highway in southern California, and I was thirty minutes late for the appointment. Five more minutes and I would have missed it altogether. The psychologist was packing up to go home, but graciously agreed to administer the tests anyway. So I entered that quiet, distraction-free room.

I pride myself on doing well on tests, regardless of what they measure. But this time, I couldn't pull myself together. My anxiety was sky high. I was slow and clumsy on spatial tasks (never my strong suit anyway), and I was sure I had scored only slightly above "idiot" on the IQ test. I was so embarrassed by my abysmal performance that I almost canceled the next appointment, when the doctor would reveal the results. But I had to know.

First, the staff psychiatrist showed me the raw scores from the testing (my IQ was well above "idiot," thank goodness). Then he droned on about vocations and options. I didn't care. I only wanted the verdict. *Yes or no? Normal or not?* Finally I asked him directly: "But do I have ADD?"

The Truth About Diagnosis

- *There is no absolute test for ADHD*

- *It's OK to get a "second opinion"*

- *A "functional diagnosis" can be made via a thorough intake interview with an ADD-savvy physician or psychologist*

- *Expect to feel relief and grief after diagnosis*

- *Not everyone has ADD – despite what you may believe*

- *Having ADD does not mean you are brain damaged*

- *Medication helps some people; expect to try several of them*

He smiled at me, almost benevolently. "Oh yes," he said. "Classic ADD."

Classic. Like a vintage car. Or a Lauren Bacall evening gown. *Classic ADD.* I liked the sound of that. Perhaps I could make peace with this ADD aberration in my brain. Dress it in a sweater twin-set and a pair of Weejuns. Make it respectable and clever.

Even better, maybe I could "fix" it so I could finally be the person I'd always wanted to be. But the only treatment I'd heard about was stimulant medication and that experiment had failed.

I needed more information, so I did some research (OK, I did a *lot* of research) about ADD, women, and possibilities. What I learned was both a pleasant surprise and a disconcerting reality.

3

ADD hot fudge sundae

It turns out that Attention Deficit / Hyperactivity Disorder (AD/HD*) comes in three delicious flavors: Hyperactive-Impulsive, Inattentive, and Combined type—a combination of the first two.

The flavors have a direct correlation to the three essentials of AD/HD—distractibility, inattention, and impulsivity.

Psychology gurus say you must have at least two of those three traits to be diagnosed with ADD and you must have had them for several years starting in childhood. Oh, and they must cause some problems in your life. (*What, like being late to your own wedding? Does that count?*)

Only a tiny fraction of adult women are solely *Hyperactive* — the drive-through, make-mine-to-go, eat-it-quick-before-it-melts type. You can recognize women with the "Big H" by the impatient sound of their ballpoint pens that clickclick-clickclick-clickclick when they're stuck in boring meetings. They're the ones who shift

*AD/HD is the correct clinical term; I use it here and elsewhere when clinical accuracy is appropriate

in their chairs every two minutes, talk circles around their co-workers, and are always in a hurry, usually running late. They have a tendency to blurt out honest —if not tactful— comments at the most inopportune moments. And they'll do anything to avoid waiting in line at the grocery store, the toll booth, or the theater.

> They say I have ADD, but—Oh look, there goes a chicken!

Predominantly Inattentive ADD women are the dreamy, creamy, slow-churned variety who prompted the T-shirt joke: "They say I have ADD, but—Oh look! There goes a chicken!" Inattentive ADD women can be found in coffee shops, staring into space while their coffee gets cold and their lunch hours (and parking meters) expire. They're excellent procrastinators and, as a result, find themselves buried hopelessly in piles of not-quite-complete paperwork, unpaid bills, and overdue library books.

Inattentive type ADD women tend to doodle during boring meetings or surreptitiously play computer games on their cell phones under the desk. Talking to an inattentive ADD woman can be an exercise in frustration: they don't seem to listen and, when they do, they often forget what's being discussed. They need constant reminders of deadlines and appointments.

Most ADD women are "Combined Type," an interesting blend of hyperactivity, impulsivity, and inattention. Combined Type ADD women can (inattentively) daydream past the exit ramp on the way to their 11 a.m. appointment and, by 1 p.m., they've overdrawn their bank accounts because they (impulsively) bought a new computer. They have trouble paying attention to hum-drum, boring tasks, but can focus for hours on a fascinating project.

Some days, Combined Type ADD women zip around town in a productive frenzy; on others, it's a monumental effort to figure out what to wear to work (assuming there are any clean clothes in the closet). Combined Type ADD women are like ADD hot fudge sundaes: alternately hot and cold, hyper-focused and distracted, energized and lethargic.

Given my toe-tappin', leg-bouncin' electricity, I'm a ringer for the ranks of "Big H" ADD — Hyperactive. I think fast. I talk fast. I move fast. But the truth is that I'm absolutely a hot fudge sundae kind of ADD woman. When my hyperactive ADD energy flags—as it does at some point in every long day—my inattentive ADD kicks into gear.

I start sentences in my head and then finish them out loud, which confuses the heck out of my husband. I daydream.

I watch mindless TV for three or four hours at a stretch. I ignore my To Do list in favor of anxiously worrying about all the things I am neglecting. I know I should be doing something, but I can't get off the sofa or the internet.

Often, my inattentive ADD creeps in when I am overwhelmed. I am paralyzed by too many choices, so my brain simply shuts down. I try to focus but I can't force myself to pay attention to anything for more than a few seconds.

Eventually, after I play with the dogs, walk in the sunshine, and regain my equilibrium, my focus improves (as much as ADD focus can improve) and my enthusiasm makes a comeback. I get off the sofa and jump into my hyperactive life again.

Of course, the delineation between inattentive and hyperactive ADD isn't neat and clean. Even in my most hyperactive moments, I am inattentive, especially to details. And in my inattentive moments, there's a little hyperactivity in play—I twirl my hair or bounce my leg or wiggle in my chair.

So what is it that goes round and round in my brain to make me run like a racehorse one minute and move like a sleepy koala the next? The experts believe it's all about the neurotransmitters (deep, mournful groan). As many times as I have read about and been told about the workings of those teeny little chemicals, I can never keep the darned neurotransmitters straight in my head (probably because my neurotransmitters aren't doing their job). So I'm writing it all down in simplified form for both of us. *Hold your breath, we're going under.* I promise it won't last long.

The section formerly known as "Let's skip this because it's gonna be boring"

My brain (and undoubtedly yours) contains 100 billion neurons (give or take a couple of billion), which are the cells that carry direct orders to our bodies. ("Move right finger .5 inches." "Breathe in. Breathe out.")

It always surprises me to be reminded that neurons are a bit like a network of fine copper wire: they conduct low-voltage electricity to speed the messages to the muscles, blood, skin, and so on. The same low-voltage current also carries more subtle messages about feelings and thoughts and plans. ("I'm sad today." "First I'll find a dress, and then I'll buy some shoes.")

Those 100 billion neurons make 200 electrical connections per second. That's like a lamp being plugged and unplugged into an outlet 200 times while you blink once. An electrical socket and plug is a nice image but a poor analogy; in our brains, the socket and plug never touch.

Our neurons make 200 connections each second!

That great brain designer in the sky decided it would be a funny joke to have little gaps in between each and every one of those 100 billion neurons. So to complete those zillion trillion circuits, the electrical surge has to jump the gap, much like Evil Knievel jumped a line of cars with his motorcycle. Medical folks call that gap the "synapse" (pronounced like a computer application gone to the dark side: *sin-apps*).

To help make sure the juice keeps flowing and the circuits connect, the great brain designer also provided some helpers: teeny chemical shuttle boats that ferry the electrical charge safely across the microscopic chasm.

The chemical ferry boats are called neurotransmitters (pronounced like a radio transmitter gone neurotic). And there are several different kinds of ferry boats/neurotransmitters. They have confusing and complicated names, so I've made them a little more friendly.

Meet the neurotransmitters

I am pleased to introduce you to Ms. Nora Penne Effrin (nor-epinephrine, also known as noradrenaline), Ms. Sarah Tonin (serotonin) and Mr. Dope A. Mean (dopamine). There are other neurotransmitters ferrying back and forth in your brain, but these three are thought to be the key players in ADD.

Ms. Effrin ("Nora" to her friends) is responsible for ensuring that we PAY ATTENTION! Ms. Tonin is the feel-good neurotransmitter; when she goes missing, depression can set in. Mr. Mean is a party animal; he's all about pleasure and fun but he's also the member of the team who handles distractibility and its lackadaisical deficit.

All three of these neurotransmitters are what scientists call "excitatory," which means they arouse your brain—as in focus, paying attention, and feeling good about life. When they play and work together nicely, there are not-too-many, not-too-few, but just the right number of them scurrying back and forth between neurons to keep your brain on an even keel.

Nora Penne Effrin

In the ADD brain, our friends the neurotransmitters have a harder time making connections. Our brains were quite literally "developmentally delayed," most likely because of some errant genetic code that our parents slipped into our chromosomes.

Sarah Tonin   "Dope" A. Mean

If you have ADD, take a look at your blood relatives; there's a good chance at least one of them had ADD, too (but they may not know it yet). ADD has a strong genetic component, which explains why many moms find out about their ADD when their children are diagnosed.

What's going on behind *your* forehead?

A lot of the credit for organizing our lives, making plans and finishing the projects (and sentences) we start goes to the prefrontal cortex of the brain; that's the big, wide part behind your forehead. Inside the prefrontal cortex, something happens called "executive function"—which always reminds me of a suit and tie (and makes me wonder: *What does that have to do with me?*).

"Executive function" sounds so straight-laced

Executive function allows us to actually follow through on our plans and to "execute" our lives in a normal, linear fashion. Words like "responsible," "reliable," "trustworthy," and "conscientious" describe excellent executive function.

The ADD brain is a few quarts low on executive function. Why? Because the neurotransmitters (those little dickens!) aren't making solid connections in the prefrontal cortex, that's why. The structure of our brains combined with the lack of neurotransmitter connections makes for a lot of static behind our foreheads.

When it's bored, the ADD brain is an unmotivated, lethargic place to hang out. But if you add an interesting experience, the ADD brain salutes and engages a bunch more norepinephrine (thanks, Nora) so it can pay attention.

With riveting stimulation, the ADD brain can go to the opposite extreme and focus on an activity for hours. Think video games, internet shopping, and your favorite TV show. That's why ADD is known as the disorder of extremes. Lack of focus one minute, hyperfocus for hours.

This is a pretty simplified view of the excruciatingly complex ADD brain. There is a lot more going on than I can understand or summarize. There is much that researchers still don't know; there are breakthroughs in brain research almost daily. In a few years, these theories will be passé and a shiny, new idea will help us understand ADD a whole lot better. In the interim, however, we at least have a few basic brain principles on board.

Variety is the spice of ADD life

ADD brains don't like being squished into neat little compartments like "Inattentive" and "Hyperactive-Impulsive"—and with good reason. Almost every ADD brain is unique; there is no other like it in the world. Dr. Steve Gordon, a psychologist from Somerset, NJ, says, "If you've met one person with ADD, you've met *one* person with ADD!"

No wonder it's so difficult to diagnose Attention Deficit Disorder. There's almost no cohesion to the symptoms. One person goes to the doctor with bankruptcy hanging over her head because she impulsively charged up her credit cards. Another person shows up because she's been put on probation at work because she can't learn the new computer system.

It's not unusual for an adult to be diagnosed with ADD by one doctor only to have the diagnosis dismissed by a second doctor who is convinced the problem is depression or bi-polar disorder or stress.

Unlike high blood pressure, you can't measure ADD with a standardized medical test. Physicians or psychologists usually start by conducting a thorough intake by asking a lot of questions; a good intake session can last up to two hours! During the intake, ADD professionals listen for stories that show long-standing distractibility or impulsivity. Sometimes they use tests to measure working memory, which is often impaired in the ADD brain. Some medical professionals order brain scans that show areas of strong or weak activity.

Ultimately, the accuracy of the diagnosis depends on the experience and knowledge of the professional (only physicians and psychologists are permitted to diagnose ADD). The uncertainty is confusing, frustrating, and time-consuming. ADD adults don't know where to turn for help, whom to believe, or what to do about their undiagnosed condition.

That was certainly true for me. Several doctors agreed that I had ADD, but my diagnosis hadn't changed anything, except perhaps to make me a little depressed that I had yet another psychological diagnosis. I seemed to be getting along OK, so I clung to a story I had read in *Driven to Distraction.*

Dr. Hallowell recalled a particular female patient who arrived for an ADD evaluation impeccably dressed and perfectly coiffed. She told Dr. Hallowell about her symptoms and, at the end of the session, waited for his decision.

He agreed that she did have ADD. With that, she thanked him and pulled on her coat. When he asked about their next appointment, she demurred, saying she didn't want treatment—she only wanted validation that she actually had ADD. He never heard from her again.

I decided to adopt her "so what" attitude toward my own ADD. Occasionally, ADD crossed my mind—like the morning my employees found me still at my desk, after working all night on a proposal that was due at noon that day. Or when I forgot to pick up my son from school. I bounced back, recovered my composure, and got my ADD back under control.

It was under control right up until I hit menopause. Or, more precisely, it hit me.

4

Midlife confessions

My midlife crisis arrived, not in the form of a shiny red Corvette, but with the sudden evaporation of my memory.

I was at the checkout counter at Macy's buying a dress when the sales clerk asked for my zip code to verify my credit card. I opened my mouth to speak, but unexpectedly I went brain dead—or "dain bread," as a friend of mine calls it. I stared at the clerk in confusion.

"I'm sorry," I mumbled. "I can't remember anything lately."

"Oh honey, I've been there," said the woman, who was probably in her late sixties. She patted my hand. "It'll get better eventually. But it's terrible to lose your mind."

Somehow, I managed to make it out of the store and to my car, where I put my head on the steering wheel and cried. This couldn't be happening to me! I had depended on my intelligence and quick wit to get by my entire life—and now they were gone! Almost overnight, I had morphed from the quickest brain in the room to a space cadet who couldn't think her way out of a paper bag.

I forgot the names of my children. I would blurt out inappropriate comments at the worst possible moments. At cocktail parties, my brain would careen off-topic during small talk. I'd notice people staring at me and I'd wonder, *What did they want? Was it my turn to say something? What were we talking about? Why was I talking to these people, anyway?*

I miss my mind. It used to be such a comfort to me

Eventually, I stopped going to business meetings because I was afraid to open my mouth; I might forget what I had planned to say. I made no new sales calls, which hurt my income. Thank goodness, I'd already closed my off-site office and had laid-off my full-time employees so I didn't have to make sensible conversation. I spoke out loud only to my dogs (who didn't mind if I forgot their names) and my husband (who minded a little more).

I got scared. Maybe this was early-onset dementia—or a brain tumor! I was certainly (and reluctantly) in the throes of menopause; my periods had stopped and hot flashes thundered through my body at the rate of fifty or sixty a day.

My youngest son asked me if I was going through "that *old* thing." *Thanks, son. I needed that!* I suppose he was right, but no one had warned me that the "old thing" would turn off the lights in my brain. There had to be more to this malfunction than age. Oh, my heavens —maybe it was my ADD roaring to life. I needed to try ADD meds again. Now!

I put in an urgent call to my psychiatrist and poured out my sad story. He listened for a few minutes and then uttered words I will never forget:

"Women's ADD brains need estrogen. Go get some."

Huh? This wasn't the answer I wanted. Just give me some pills so I can get back to normal again. Besides, what the heck did estrogen have to do with ADD? Well, quite a lot, as I learned over the next few months.

Those lovely 'mones

Estrogen is a kissing cousin to those three famous neurotransmitters we learned about in Chapter 3. (If you don't remember meeting Nora Penne Effrin, Dope A. Mean, and Sarah Tonin, please go back and introduce yourself—they're pretty interesting!)

I'm not sure how they figured this out, but the research folks say that estrogen sits on the "receptor site" of our female neurons. When estrogen is at its most robust, it acts like the chemical equivalent of sticky pine tar in a catcher's mitt, snagging those neurotransmitters as they ferry across the little gap (the synapse, remember?). Our brain's electrical system makes excellent connections and all is well in the cognitive performance arena. We remember where we parked the car.

"Come to Mama!"

When estrogen goes missing (as it does every month during our menstrual cycles and permanently at menopause), there's no catcher on the receptor site yelling "Come to Mama!" So those little neurotransmitters have more trouble docking on the other side. The electrical connections get a little frizzled and we get a little frazzled. We interrupt ourselves in mid-sentence and perhaps take a detour to the lingerie store when we should be going to the dry cleaners.

Estrogen ebb and flow impacts the brains of all women, but sneak ADD into the picture and the effect quadruples. Even the best ADD meds can't compensate for a lack of estrogen catcher's mitts. Low estrogen means high ADD symptoms. That's why ADD seems to get worse right before your period (when there's no estrogen on board) and why it gets so much better during pregnancy (when there is a bumper crop of estrogen).

Somewhere in between making-babies-time and menopause is perimenopause. During perimenopause (which can start as early as ten years before the real-deal menopause), our estrogen does a flirty, flamboyant fan dance. She flutters behind her fan for a while, withholding her juicy goodness, and then changes her mind and parades in full regalia through our bodies. When she parades, our ADD seems to get much better; when she flutters, it gets worse than ever. Up and down. Better and worse. The only parallel to this estrogen roller coaster is in adolescence, when our hormones control our moods, lust, and attention.

Ms. Estrogen does her fan dance

It was starting to make sense. I had been diagnosed with ADD at age forty-five, on the cusp of perimenopause. My body had been reacting to alternately overflowing estrogen followed by an estrogen drought. My brain, which had been hanging on by its neurotransmitter fingernails, was overwhelmed by the hormonal disruption, and my ADD emerged—front and center. ADD really *does* get worse with age.

But the thought of taking estrogen? Oh, no; not this woman. I'd read all that scary stuff about the Women's Health Initiative, the largest study of hormone replacement therapy ever conducted. I was not enthused about setting up fertile ground for breast cancer or heart problems. So I tried soy isoflavonoids (whatever the heck those are), acupuncture, herbal supplements, and even "natural" hormones. Nothing worked well or for very long.

I couldn't go on like this. By a small miracle, I found a doctor who had a dual specialty in gynecology and psychiatry. Although it took her almost a year to convince me, I finally agreed to try estrogen patches. That was another miracle. Within a few weeks, I felt more confident about my ability to rub two words together and make a coherent sentence. I wasn't at full strength, but I was running at right about 40 percent—a huge improvement.

[My choice to use hormone replacement therapy isn't for every woman. I tell people I am a walking, talking science experiment and by the time I find out that I did the wrong thing, it will be

too late. But I have made peace with the consequences of my decision. And as the gynecologist/psychiatrist observed: "This is a quality of life issue."]

Is it A.D.D. or A.G.E.?

By this time, I'd done a lot of internet surfing trying to sort out the menopause symptoms (the A.G.E.) from the attention deficit symptoms (the A.D.D.). They looked darned similar: memory problems, foggy brain, distractibility, sleep disruption. My ADD didn't cause my hot flashes, of course. And my A.G.E. wasn't responsible for my tardiness. But a lot of my female friends told me they thought they had developed a late-life case of ADD; they were "dain bread" too. It seemed that into every menopause a little ADD must fall. But for my friends, the symptoms didn't last. For me, they were eternal.

"Into every menopause a little ADD must fall."

The dividing line between A.G.E. and A.D.D. is longevity of symptoms. My friends had been able to focus, finish projects, and balance their checkbooks before menopause. They had also been successful in their careers, raised fine families, and managed their lives in a way I envied.

I often compare my over-age-forty ADD diagnosis to changing one piece of data in a computer program. Even though it's a small change, it forces a reset of *all* the data, backward and forward. And when I looked back at my life with the new ADD line of code, I was overcome with sadness, regret, and a touch of anger.

If only I had known this when I was younger! I could have gotten treatment and been able to focus on and finish *my* projects. I could have raised *my* fine family and managed *my* life better. I could have learned how to make outlines and follow them. I could have be on time to work every morning. I could have used the thousands of minutes I'd wasted on ADD during my "one wild and precious life" to create a better life, not only for me, but for my family.

So the question was: Is there still time to live the life I'd dreamed of, that I had tried again and again to achieve? I was fifty. How many more chances would I get in this life? I needed to make some decisions and do something.

Yet I hung back, caught in the grip of indecision. *Should I spin my advertising agency back to life? Should I go back to school? Was my aging brain even capable of studying? How would I compensate for my ADD now that I wasn't quite as quick on the uptake as I had been in my thirties and forties?*

Then there were the bigger questions: *Who am I? Why am I taking up space on the planet? Why now? What is my purpose?*

Sometimes, before you can move forward, you first have to back up for a reality check. In my previous life, I had made choices without including my ADD. This time, I wanted to hug my demons before they bit me in the behind; I wanted to work with my ADD instead of fighting it.

My years in therapy had taught me well: The only way to deal with a difficult issue is to plow straight through. My ADD had been with me from the beginning. To learn how best to live with it today, I needed to rewind the clock on my life and take a new look, using the lens of ADD.

5

A (D) Diva is born

*Y*ou always get your way!

Who, me? As a child, I was indignant at my younger brother's accusation. He must have been jealous or delusional. In my mind, it was quite the opposite: I was doing things everybody's way *but* mine.

Admittedly, I did "boss him around" a lot. My moods were mercurial. Within the span of an hour, I'd shower him with affection, then indifference, then anger, and then affection again. And when I needed some precious time alone, I'd lock him out of my room. I suppose I *was* a high-maintenance sibling.

Now that I have some distance from that difficult era and an adult's perspective, I realize that my brother might have been right—but for the wrong reasons. He (and my parents and teachers and the rest of the world) completely misunderstood my motives. I wasn't deliberately selfish or unkind. I was trying my level best to manage something weird and strange that lived inside me; a nameless force that set me apart from everyone else. In my childish and clumsy way, I was trying to control my unsuspected ADD.

Dr. Patricia Quinn, a developmental pediatrician in the Washington, DC area who writes frequently about girls and women with AD/HD, reports that ADD symptoms in young girls are quite different than they are in boys. Hyperactive ADD girls can talk excessively, interrupt, and have trouble waiting their turns. They may have emotional highs and lows or even temper tantrums. They jump quickly from one activity to another and they tend to be *(ahem)* quite bossy.

Inattentive ADD girls often have trouble following directions and paying attention. They may appear to lack motivation and have difficulty starting and finishing tasks. Combined-type ADD girls have traits from both sides of the aisle, which was a perfect description of my childhood.

I had no trouble initiating interesting tasks—I was constantly starting new hobbies—but monotonous household chores were, well, a chore, so I avoided them as much as possible. My family's strong work ethic was instilled in me at an early age, but I was easily pulled off task which was dangerously close to being "lazy."

There was no mystery about my moods, which trilled up and down the scales from low C to high A; I wore my heart on my sleeve. I was also ultra-sensitive to criticism; my feelings would wilt at the hint of a scowl or a harsh word.

I wore my heart on my sleeve

I was constantly reprimanded for being too boisterous, for talking out of turn and for "flopping around" on the furniture. In an era when little girls were expected to sit quietly, speak softly and act like a lady, I was a defiant free spirit. I was rebellious, creative, and opinionated—none of which earned me any Brownie points with adults (or, as I later learned, to other children).

After a few painful episodes of disapproval and subsequent isolation, I learned to stifle my natural exuberance in the presence of others. I spent a lot of time alone, reading, daydreaming and berating myself for my social faux pas. I vowed to do better "next time."

But taming an ADD brain like mine wasn't as simple as reining in my sassy retorts. My brain raced at 225 miles per hour; even *I* could barely keep up with it. Before I could put on the brakes, I would step into a new and improved puddle of behavioral doo-doo. It was quite discouraging and it cost me a lot of friendships.

I clamped down harder on my speed-demon brain, to the point that I was consciously controlling almost every public expression or action. And as I implemented super-control over my brain, I also began to over-control the rest of my environment.

My Nancy Drew books had to be alphabetized by title. I adamantly refused to wear clothing that was itchy or harsh on my skin. I demanded time alone so I could get away from the rigors of the outside world and rekindle my energy for another day of "fitting in." It sounds like a "step on a crack, break your mother's back" kind of obsession. But I wasn't obsessed; I was overwhelmed and exhausted.

Between my ADD tendencies and my efforts to mitigate them, I am sure I came across as the worst kind of diva: self-absorbed and petulant, demanding that people cater to her every whim. But there is a world of difference between a true diva, who is capriciously temperamental, and an ADDiva like me, who is working overtime simply to keep herself upright and functional.

Divalicious

A dyed-in-the-wool diva has an unquestioning sense of entitlement. She believes her desires are always the highest priority, no matter how unreasonable. She is grandiose and careless about the effect of her stringent demands. What people think of her is decidedly unimportant; leaving a trail of resentment goes with the territory. A true diva creates her world to satisfy her extreme self-interest.

True divas have a sense of entitlement; ADDivas don't

ADDivas, by contrast, create our worlds strictly for self-preservation. We are dancing as fast as we can to meet the demands of the outside world—not our own desires. We are preoccupied (which can look a lot like haughtiness or snob-bery) because we are trying to vanquish the tempest in our heads. We monitor our words and behavior in a fierce attempt to meet the standards of a world that is as alien to us as outer space is to earthworms.

As an ADDiva, my brother's accusations of selfishness made no sense to me. *Of course* I needed things to be "my way" because I was trying to keep my head above water. But all that flailing apparently splashed a lot of water in his direction, and undoubtedly he suffered because of my ADD brain. It grieves me to know that I caused him pain. Without some kind of out-side assistance, however, I doubt that I could have done any-thing differently. My ADD diagnosis was decades in the future.

As I matured, my divalicious behaviors moderated somewhat, although you'd never prove that by my ex-husband. He was convinced I was the original drama queen, as evidenced by my mood swings from the depths of pessimism ("With God as my witness, I'll *never* be happy again!") to the heights of ecstasy ("Everything's coming up roses!"). Honestly, I did feel a bit like I was at the end of a bull whip, flung here and there by my strong emotions. But I had no idea how to stop them from swamping my life at regular intervals (or more accurately, at irregular intervals).

The ADD brain is a playground for emotions. Tantalizing research suggests that we have normal emotions, but since we have trouble keeping a lid on them, they are expressed in extremes. We lash out in anger instead of calmly stating our position; we cry in frustration instead of making a reasonable

The ADDiva emotional roller coaster

request; we hold a grudge instead of granting forgiveness. Our emotional outbursts only add more credence to our "drama queen" label.

I suspect that some of my roller-coaster moods can be attributed to hormones. My ADD took alternate turns for the better or worse depending on my monthly allocation of estrogen. Immediately before my period, I would sink into a Chicken Little state of mind, absolutely persuaded that the sky would fall at any moment. Three days later, I was a changed woman, revving up for another optimistic charge toward my goals.

Let the diva focus!

There is another, equally compelling rationale for my ADD drama queen status: drama keeps my brain engaged so I can focus! As I write these words, it sounds absurd that I would deliberately choose conflict or drama as a way of life. Yet, at points in my life, I have lived from one crisis to the next with barely a minute to breathe between them.

When the ADD brain perks up its attention ears, those little neurotransmitter ferry boats rev up their motors and do a much more efficient job of delivering the electrical charge between our billions of neurons. Our brains function better with a full charge. Our executive function actually functions and we get things accomplished, we feel happier and life is good.

But there can be a dramatic price exacted from our *grande'* shot of adrenaline (Ms. Nora Penn Effrin) and dopamine (Dope A. Mean) when we use tension and drama to force our brains to *think fast*: chronic stress. During my drama queen days, I developed tension headaches, irregular heartbeat, stomach ailments, and pain in my jaw from clenching my teeth. Most of the time I was worn out from riding the bucking bronco that kept me alert.

Now that I know more about my ADD, my level of drama has subsided (although we might want to check with my husband for outside validation). But I do retain some of the traits of a "do it my way" diva: I need my clothes hung in color order in my closet so I can find my black turtleneck without using too much precious attention. I alphabetize my spices and label my refrigerator shelves. All these idiosyncrasies are coping strategies I use to accommodate my ADD.

For the most part, I keep them to myself. I covertly install atomic clocks in every room so there is a higher likelihood that I will be on time for appointments. I reserve specific locations for my piles that are not to be disturbed by anyone but me. But I don't live in a vacuum. Occasionally, Victor will inadvertently stumble into one of my sacred rules and we have words. He now knows not to move my car keys, even if they're in the laundry room!

ADD cuts a wide swath through our lives, but in its wake, there is an effervescent perspective that is sorely needed. Certainly, we ADDivas are often late, distracted, disorganized, and impulsive—but in our midst are some of the most honest, loyal, compassionate, creative, and generous women alive. We aren't true divas; we're pseudo-divas!

I regard the term "ADDiva" as a sign of my enthusiasm and vibrancy. I don my whimsical, pink-polka-dot ADDiva hat as a reminder to take life not-too-seriously, to roll with the punches, and to wear my ADD proudly.

6

Flit like a butterfly

I don't get it," I told my husband one sunny Saturday afternoon. "I can understand the hyperactivity and impulsivity, but these ADD books keep talking about being distracted. I'm not distracted."

It was involuntary; Victor couldn't censor himself fast enough. He laughed. *Laughed.*

To understand the seriousness of this offense, you must know that I hate being laughed at; it's right up there with singing off-key in public on the Torture Hit Parade. I fall into shame, I want to hide, and then I get ticked off—all in a blink.

Being an exceedingly smart guy and knowing me better than any-one in the world, Victor instantly recognized the cycle ... and the deep hole he had dug for himself. He made a quick recovery. "I'm not laughing *at* you, sweetie," he said, pulling me close to him. "I'm laughing *with* you." Strange. I wasn't laughing *at all*.

"OK, let me explain," he said. "You tell me you are going to the garden to pick green beans. You go to the shed to get a basket, but a few minutes later, you come out with the hoe and a package of cucumber seeds. You uncover the bed for the cucumbers and plant one row, but then you start watering the tomatoes. Then, while the hose is still running, you go back into the shed to get some fertilizer so you can fertilize the squash. This goes on for a couple of hours, and you still haven't picked the green beans!"

I was stunned. *That* was distractibility? I assumed everyone started several jobs at once and made a round-robin affair of them: hoeing, then watering, then harvesting, then weeding, then back to hoeing.

"But I *did* pick the green beans; I came back around to them after I did all that other stuff. I was multi-tasking," I said, triumphantly. "I do it all the time!"

"Oh, I know you do it all the time!" Even from inside a cuddle, Victor's voice sounded darned judgmental. "That's just who you are!"

I knew he was right. I do flit from one task to another, much like the gorgeous swallowtail butterflies that float from blossom to blossom in my back yard. They land on a white flower and drink deeply, and then abruptly turn their attention to a purple flower, and then return to the white. I wonder what goes through those tiny butterfly minds as they flit and float; their only task is to nourish their delicate little bodies.

I, however, have a zillion jobs. My focus jumps from answering email to calling the exterminator to coaching a client—or whatever comes into my line of sight. Or hearing. Or head. I bounce from one room to another, run from one project to another and madly scribble down one idea after another so they don't escape. Somehow, distractibility looks more graceful on butterflies.

Back in the early days ...

I've been this way since I was a toddler. My mom recalls that I would drag out some blocks, build a few towers, and then tend my baby dolls in their pink bassinet. After I'd put the dolls down for their naps, I'd shift to reading some Little Golden books (which had no business aligned neatly on the shelves, but were happier scattered all over the floor).

Then it was time for dress-up; I would pull out my mother's discarded necklaces and long dresses and parade around the house. By the time my dad came in for dinner, he'd look around and wonder if a tornado had hit the house. Nope. It was just li'l ole me, doing my ADD thing ... or whatever they called it at the time (I suspect they called it "messy"). I never learned the "clean up your room" lesson; I got distracted by my own toys in the process!

This environment of spontaneous disarray was a fertile incubator for my imagination and creativity. Many kudos go to my mother for her encouragement (or tolerance), but it couldn't have been easy.

She must have empathized with the mother of Little Billy in the long-running Sunday comic strip *Family Circus*. The cartoon mom would send Billy on a simple errand in the neighborhood. A fat dotted line in the cartoon traced his distracted path across yards and streets. He'd make a quick visit to a friendly dog, pick up a shiny penny, climb a tree, splash in a puddle, and discover an old kite. By the time he arrived back at home, he had forgotten the purpose of his errand.

Even as an adult, I am much like Little BIlly: I'm endlessly fascinated by bright, shiny objects that cause a short circuit in my memory. I ignore the goal and take a detour, distracted by something, *anything,* that is more compelling.

Last year, the battery on my van died. After the auto club guy jump-started it, he told me to let it recharge by running the engine for about fifteen minutes. *Seven hours later,* I remembered that my van was still running.

In the meantime, I had fed the dogs, taken a shower, talked to my assistant, written a blog post, and completed a half-dozen other tasks on my To Do list. The van wasn't even on my To Do list; that was something I thought I'd remember (*silly girl!*).

Distractible/attractible

Distractibility is one of the Big Three on the ADD diagnostic hit parade, a sure sign that there is a malfunction in our executive function. We leave mayonnaise jars uncapped, emails half-written, and skirt hems held up with tape instead of thread.

The simple reason is that our attention wanders—which, as the experts say, "results in extreme difficulty maintaining focus." Mr. Dope A. Mean (dopamine) is primarily responsible for distractibility (or for regular folks, single-mindedness). He toys with our pre-frontal cortex, teasing it into focus, but only for a moment. The more interesting or challenging the task, the more often Mr. Mean will stick around and help make those all-important electrical jumps across the synapse to complete our brain circuits. Of course, the exact opposite is also true: repetitive tasks don't hold much sway with Mr. Mean. He dozes and we get distracted or bored.

For instance, I can perform tedious work like sorting paper clips or filing bills for only a short time before I want to jump out of my skin. I get antsy, stressed, and irritable. At that point, I can be distracted by almost anything that is only marginally more interesting.

Even when I embark on an interesting task, full of verve and enthusiasm, boredom can set in at pivotal points: on the fourteenth step of a thirty-step project; when I am forced to wait while my computer installs automatic updates; or when a stubborn problem refuses multiple, massive efforts at a solution. A "normal" brain might take a break, come back refreshed, and jump in again. My frustrated ADDiva brain takes a break and never returns. That causes some, shall we say, *challenges* with completion, which is also known as *getting things done*.

Deadlines are my friend

D-o-n-e is my favorite four-letter word, but I seldom get to use it. Given an unspecified amount of time to finish a project, I can meander down dozens of distracted pathways that do *not* move the project forward. I love to gather information (it's new, it's interesting, it keeps my attention) and the internet makes it far too easy for me to lose hours digging around in obscure sites that have precious little to do with my task.

When I realize, with a start, that I've wasted the entire afternoon, I try to kick my brain back into high gear. But that lasts only a little while—until the due date is imminent. Then the urgency of the situation wakes up my bored and sleepy brain, snapping those sluggish neurotransmitters back into action.

The best inspiration, as they say, is a deadline. That's why a lot of ADD folks work in deadline-driven occupations: graphic design, journalism, law enforcement. In my case, it was radio and TV news and advertising, all of which have tight deadlines and therefore provide high stimulation.

> A lot of ADD folks work in deadline-driven occupations

In an interesting paradox, brain experts report that when ADD folks are pressured to perform by someone else (a boss, a spouse, a client), they actually do worse on tasks, especially with a strict time limit (a deadline). When the stakes are high—a graduate school exam or job interview, for instance—ADD brains are likely to shut down, paralyzed by the importance of the event.

I suspect the difference is familiarity: day-to-day job deadlines are expected. One-time events that can change the course of our lives are more stressful. We don't have a chance to be "engaged" or interested in the task; we are far too worried about doing the job perfectly.

The perfection connection

Perfectionism. Now, there's a good reason I'm a 95 percent kind of gal. I can breeze through the fresh, interesting part of a project. Most of the time, I can even steel myself to plow through the drab midsection. But when I'm on the downward slope with the finish line in view, my ADD-induced anxiety rekindles.

I've lived the nightmare of misplaced decimal points and misspelled words so many times that I second-guess myself, reviewing the entire project. I dream of having time to throw it all away and start over. Or at the very least to have time for major revisions.

If I rewrite the article just once more, I'm sure it will be ready to submit. Oh, maybe I need to change the first paragraph and then it will be fine. Oh, look, here's some more information that would spice it up a bit. But now the new first paragraph doesn't work. Maybe I should change the introduction.

This little exercise can go on endlessly—with or without a deadline, to be honest—which leaves me, oh, say about 95 percent complete. I just can't push through to the finale until I'm sure it's perfect. Which isn't going to happen. Cue the deadline so I can get d-o-n-e.

Of course, there are things that must be done "perfectly." Taxes, for instance. The tax people are not amused if you skip lines 14 and 23; and when the IRS says April 15 is the deadline, they mean it. There are consequences for ignoring their rigid rules (unless you file an extension, which is a universally accepted ADDiva delay). Not surprisingly, filing taxes is one of our least favorite jobs. We tend to procrastinate. A lot. Because taxes aren't very interesting. Plus, they're linear with lots of tiny numbers. So we procrastinate a little more.

Just do it. Or not.

Non-ADD folks (known in some circles as "normal") tell us we need to develop more self-discipline. "Well, who wouldn't prefer to do interesting things all the time?" they exclaim, voices dripping with sarcasm. "We all have to do things that are boring, so buck up. Stiff upper lip. When the going gets tough, the tough get going. Just *do* it!"

Wow, I'd never thought of that before! I guess I should just put a little willpower into it and try a little harder. I could change my name to "The Little Engine That Could." *Gotta do it. Gotta do it. Gotta do it.* Sorry, I stumbled into a bit of sarcasm myself.

The Little Engine Who Couldn't

Trust me, if ADDivas could use sheer willpower successfully, we'd ramp up the engines and push harder than any little choo-choo train. But we've already tried "Just Do It," *ad nauseum.* It make us less effective, more stressed, and a little crazy. No matter how much we want it to work, it doesn't.

Make no mistake, losing interest and falling short of completion are not the same as giving up. ADDivas are not quitters! Quite the opposite is true: we are tenacious almost to a fault. And we *do* complete projects in our own good time. Take it from my eighty-five-year-old mother, who recently told me the story of her pink mittens.

"When I was in high school, Aunt Laura bought me some yarn to knit a sweater," she said. "Remember how tight she was with money? Well, that yarn cost one dollar, and she didn't want to waste her money, so she made me promise to finish the sweater. Oh, I promised I'd finish it!

"I got the front of that sweater done and the back of it down to the ribbing. Then I stopped. I went to college, and it sat there on the knitting needles for ten years.

How does a sweater become a pair of mittens? ADD!

"When I got pregnant with you, I unraveled the whole sweater and made myself a pair of mittens. Most people would have made baby booties, but heck, someone had already given me a pair of baby booties! I didn't need booties and I had a lot of fun making those mittens!"

I love the way my mother listened to her heart instead of bending to pressure from miserly old Aunt Laura. And I vividly remember those pink mittens; she wore them for years. I had no idea they were supposed to be her sweater or my baby booties.

Her story makes an important point. We can complete things by simply moving the finish line. Some of the things on my To Do list get "done" because the opportunity to do them expires (it's too late to plant flowers when there is snow on the ground!). I can make the conscious choice to delete some of the things on my list that I once deemed highly important but that have become trivial over time. We can literally change the meaning of "done" to a definition that works for our ADD brains.

We can plan to flit from task to task, like those beautiful swallowtail butterflies. We can drop our own version of "breadcrumbs" (stick-on notes? labels?) along the way so eventually we can find our way back to that first task.

And when we work "round robin," the tomatoes get a drink, the cucumbers are planted and we enjoy green beans for supper. *Tomorrow* night.

D-O-N-E is my favorite four-letter word

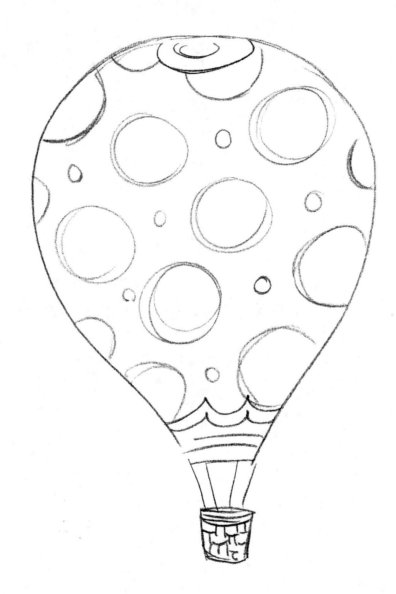

7

The answer is always YES

The spring I turned fifty-three, I bought a hot air balloon. "You did WHAT?" my son exclaimed when I called him the next day. "I've never known anyone who bought a hot air balloon, Mom!"

Neither had I. Yet it made perfect sense in the moment, despite the fact that:

1. I am terrified of heights;
2. I didn't know how to fly a hot air balloon; and
3. I'd never laid eyes on the balloon I was buying.

But I bought it, anyway. Of course. It's ADD. Impulsive ADD.

To be fair, I waited a few days before I committed to the purchase. I did some due diligence and almost backed out (and I later wished I had followed that instinct!). But the appeal was irresistible—I'd use the balloon for my women's retreats, to encourage women to soar to their fullest potential, literally defying gravity. I'd name the balloon *Passionate Possibility,* after my new company. It would be inspiring and meaningful.

For months, hot air balloons filled my thoughts and guided my actions. I found an instructor who agreed to teach me to fly. I went to the annual balloon rally in Anderson, SC and helped crew a balloon race. I borrowed money to buy a fifteen-passenger van and a tilting hitch rack to hold the balloon basket (the envelope travels inside the van). I learned about propane tanks and inflation fans and cold packing the balloon. The first (and only) time we inflated that huge, multi-colored balloon, I was speechless with pride and awe.

The end of my story is far less exciting. The balloon turned out to be defective and would never be airborne. The guy who sold it to me was an extremely clever con artist who'd had nine lawsuits filed against him (my due diligence hadn't included a criminal check). I didn't learn to fly, and I didn't add balloon rides to my retreats.

But even as I mourned the loss of my money, my balloon, and its promise, there was a whisper in the back of my mind that said, "Yeah, but you bought a hot air balloon! How cool is that!"

I've put the balloon episode behind me now, but "Yes" continues to be one of my favorite words. I've said "Yes" to scuba diving, brain exercises, glass blowing, bird watching, ballet dancing and dozens more fascinating endeavors. Some of them have stayed with me; most of them ended up on the cutting room floor of my life. But I was glad to have sampled them, if only for a short while.

Blame it on the brain

The ADD killjoys will say I am merely living up to my impulsive and hyperactive billing. Impulsivity is, of course, one of the clues psychiatrists look for when diagnosing ADD. They call it a "lack of inhibition," which loosely translates to saying "Go for it!" when "Let's stop and think this over" would be a better answer.

The culprit, as usual, is that darned prefrontal cortex. It's the air traffic controller of our minds, directing some of our actions to stay in a holding pattern while granting permission to a selected few to come in for a landing. At least, that's how it works in the linear brain.

In the ADD brain, Ms. Prefrontal Cortex takes a lot of coffee breaks (probably because caffeine works part-time as an

attention booster). In her absence, the floodgates open and I run amuck on impulsivity. I'm sure she was out for a latte' when I matter-of-factly informed a prospective advertising client that the name of her new apartment building reminded me of a pregnancy clinic. You could have heard a pin drop after that impromptu pronouncement. I'm surprised the client didn't walk out of the meeting. Curse you, Ms. Prefrontal Cortex, for exiting the building when I needed you most!

Our "let's say yes" approach is a two-pronged ADD issue. First, it reflects the absence of "let's say no" thanks to a lethargic Ms. Prefrontal Cortex; and second, it gives us loads of stimulation ("it's new!" "it's different!" "it's interesting!") so that we have an excuse to pay attention. I was a fan of Number Two for years, apparently to the point of excess.

"Going overboard"

My father called it "going overboard," as in "There goes Linda, going overboard again!" He might have been thinking about my short stint as a Girl Scout when I earned all the merit badges in one year. Or the summer I spent my allowance on a pink papier-mâché ice cream freezer and made hand-churned ice cream every single day.

 I never thought that "going overboard" was such a bad thing, although I'm sure that my dad said it to discourage me from my over-the-top activities. It puts a smile in my heart to be curious and adventuresome.

Today, I "go overboard" on bird feeders (we have forty-seven of them) and black, long-sleeved T-shirts (I have eleven, all identical, all half price) and storage containers (you can never have too many). When I go overboard on shopping, I often go overboard on returning the stuff I bought, too. I'm on a first-name basis with the customer service clerks at my favorite stores.

Euphemisms for "going overboard"

Taking on more than you can handle.
Biting off more than you can chew.
Spreading yourself too thin.
Too many balls in the air.
Lots of irons in the fire.
You have a lot going on.
Burning the candle at both ends.

But I *like* going overboard; it keeps me open to new possibilities. Clinging to childlike wonder about the world is a good thing. And now that I'm older, I've decided I owe it to myself to explore every nook and cranny. After all, I have only a few decades left on this planet, and I plan to leave with a pocket full of wonderful experiences.

Without some kind of moderation, however, saying "Yes!" to balloons, t-shirts, and careless words has consequences. If I blurt out unkind words, I also endure the backlash of anger. When I shop online too often, my credit card screams for mercy. If I take on too many tantalizing commitments, I can't do justice to any of them.

It's like the guy on the old Ed Sullivan Show who was a professional plate spinner (now I ask you, what kind of job is *that* to put on your resume?). At first, he jiggled just a few of them on top of tall, skinny poles; then he added more and more plates, running back and forth to make sure none of them stopped spinning.

I'm not a professional plate spinner

I'm a darned good plate spinner, but I'm not a pro. I say "Yes!" to more and more pretty plates, but I know that at some point, I won't be able to keep up the pace. Some of those plates will fall to the ground and shatter.

There's no one to blame but myself. I'm the one who adds more and more plates, who paints herself into miserably tight corners. My ADD pre-frontal cortex can't prioritize the important To Dos on my list, so they get jumbled into a heap of crises.

Often, I am so burdened by the sheer number of things that need my full attention that I'm like the deer in the headlights, paralyzed by indecision. I am stuck. But even when I don't prioritize or make decisions, I do make subconscious choices about which plates I will keep spinning and which one I will allow to fall. Not deciding IS a decision. It's just not a deliberate or purposeful decision, which can cause serious consequences.

I know I should say "no" occasionally, or breathe slowly before I speak, or set limits on my spending. But I also know my resolution won't last for long. My *joie de vivre* (also known as "coffee breaks for Ms. Cortex") will break through and I'll be back in the straits of overwhelm.

Just
SAY
NO

When I reach the pinnacle of over-commitment and my brain wiring develops a short circuit, I think back to Mrs. Savage and my high school Latin class. Mrs. Savage taught us about Terence, a Roman playwright from the first century B.C. who wrote: "Moderation in all things." I suspect moderation is absent from my DNA, perhaps pushed aside by the genetics of ADD.

To me, moderation is exceedingly bland, like wearing sensible shoes and eating the same food for lunch every day. Where are the highs and lows, the white-hot passion and the melancholy blues? Oh yes, they live in the hearts of ADDivas!

I did some research on good old Terence and found that he was a comedic dramatist. He wrote comedies! He might well have been the forerunner of today's "Comedy Channel." His admonition about moderation might have been a joke! Wouldn't that be a kick in the pants, if the ancient wisdom we solemnly take to heart was intended to be tongue-in-cheek?

Now that would be an ADD happy ending—and my permission slip to keep right on going overboard.

Permission slip

This grants _____

the right to continue going overboard

as long as she remembers to

take care of herself, too.

expires at the end of a fascinating life

Step away from the piles
and no one gets hurt!

8

Professional disorganizer

*H*ey, why is my phone number on this Post-it?"

Erica, the woman I had called in desperation to help me clear out my clutter, held up a yellow scrap of paper—and I crumpled with shame. My psychiatrist (the genius who had first diagnosed me) had given me a couple of names of professional organizers. I had misplaced the note at the bottom of a laundry basket full of papers that I had stashed in my husband's office. The note had been buried there for *two years*.

I confessed, fully expecting the organizer to roll her eyes and sigh. Instead, she giggled. Then I giggled. Then we laughed. Too funny. Too ridiculous. Too ADD-ish. Later, she told me that I was the most ADD client she'd ever worked with in the twelve years she'd been a professional organizer. I wasn't sure whether to be insulted or proud, but I took it as a compliment and we laughed some more.

Sometimes, it takes a sense of humor and a few belly laughs to get through those ADD piles.

We ADD women need our piles. We are so afraid we'll lose something in a drawer or a folder ("out of sight, certainly out of the ADD mind") that we keep everything out in the open where we can see it.

But after a couple of days, we can't see the important stuff anyway, because it's buried under the new stuff we don't want to lose. Unless we sort through it, phone numbers can get lost for, oh, at least a couple of years. (By the way, I had no idea Erica had been one of the organizers my psychiatrist had recommended; an ADD coach had given me her name again, one week before we met.)

Hiring a professional organizer wasn't easy for me. It rattled around in my brain with the "F" word: Failure. Failure to be a good wife, failure to be a good role model for my children, failure to be a real woman. Outwardly, I dismissed the absurdly old-fashioned notion that a woman's merit is measured by the glow on her hardwood floors. But the nagging voice of my 1950s upbringing pinned me against her pointy, Playtex bosom and demanded that I find a place for everything

and put everything in its place. I had to admit, there were
some persuasive arguments in her favor.

In the clutter gutter

Disorganization is expensive for me. I lost the contract for
writing a magazine article twice and was too embarrassed
to ask for it a third time, so I didn't get paid. When I cleaned
my car, a week before I traded it in, I found an uncashed
paycheck that was eight months old. I've lost prescriptions for
ADD medications, tickets to a play, and receipts for rebates.

Clutter has caused me physical injury, too. I was picking my
way through a narrow path of "stuff" in the garage at my
women's retreat house and caught my shoe on a beautiful,
scrolled planter that was sitting in the walkway; I fell straight
into the concrete, cracked two ribs, and broke my wrist. It
still hurts to think about it.

And then there's the simple aggravation of not being able
to find things when I need them. When I am ready for the
weed eater and it has "myst-appeared" (as my children used
to say), I lose precious time digging through the garage, the
garden shed, and the attic. If I don't find it, sometimes I will

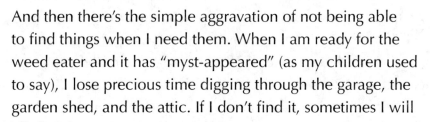

buy another one, which is also added expense. And the time I lose searching for missing objects is gone forever.

A researcher has compiled data that shows even if we spend only five minutes looking for our car keys each day, it adds up to 30 hours a year. Multiply that by an 80-year life span (subtracting a few years when we were too young to drive) and it means we spend 13 weeks of our lives finding those car keys. And I have been known to spend a lot more than five minutes locating my other earring or prescription.

The truth is, clutter drives me batty. I swear, ordinary household objects silently scream at me as I walk by: "Put me in the dishwasher!" "I need to be painted and I need new knobs!" "Call the repair guy so I can stop leaking!" "There's something important at the bottom of this pile!"

I don't stop to take care of those things in the moment because my brain is already overloaded from thousands of other silent screams: "You need to upload the new webinar to your website!" "Can't you be on time for once?" "These pants are too tight; you need to go on a diet!" Of course, everybody has these little screaming meemies in their heads, but most people are able to discard the fluff and focus on what's important. My brain doesn't work that way. I have to make a conscious effort to quiet the madding crowd.

Perhaps I should try the threatening tactics of Pippi Long-stocking, the irrepressible Swedish heroine in a series of books I adored as a child. One day, Pippi (who I am sure would qualify for an ADD diagnosis today) was looking for her hat, which had "myst-appeared."

> ... At last she even looked on the hat shelf, but there was nothing there except a frying pan, a screwdriver and a piece of cheese.
>
> "There's no order in here at all, and you can't find a single thing," said Pippi disgustedly, "though to be sure, I have missed this piece of cheese for a long time and it's lucky it turned up at last."
>
> "Hey, Hat," she shrieked, "are you going shopping or aren't you? If you don't come out this minute, it will be too late."
>
> No hat came out.

Pippi Longstocking had a messy house

"Well then, it can blame itself if it's so stupid, but I don't want to hear any complaining," she said sternly.

My hat doesn't respond to my threats, either. Nor do my keys, my purse, my shoes, or my laptop. They repose in silence, giggling silently because they have hidden themselves so cleverly amid my clutter.

There are several kinds of clutter in my house. There is Important Clutter—things I don't want to forget, so I must have them in plain view. There is the Unfiled Clutter—stuff I don't have time (or desire) to put away. And then there is Procrastination Clutter—the stuff I don't know what to do with and can't make a decision about, so I put it in a ... pile.

Erica helped me see that most of my kitchen clutter was Procrastination Clutter (my words, not hers). We set about creating workable solutions. I had no place to put away all those receipts and important papers and magazines.

Rummaging in my attic, we found an inexpensive rolling cart with lots of skinny drawers. I had bought the cart six months earlier because it looked so neat and organized—two adjectives I aspired to emulate. Alas! I had never found the perfect place for the cart, so it had been stashed out of sight until the right occasion emerged. This *was* the right occasion.

We assembled the cart and nestled it into a corner of my kitchen between the wastebasket and recycling bin. Then we labeled each of the skinny drawers: "Action items," "Bills," "Receipts," and so on.

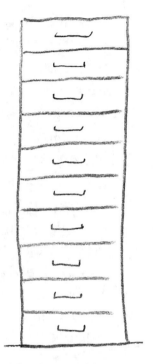

The skinny little cart system with its legible labels would have worked great if I had actually used it. I started off with great ambition, so for a few weeks there were fewer piles on the counters and kitchen table. I didn't mind putting stuff into the drawers, but I hated filing it (refer to "out of sight, out of mind"). Mostly, it was Erica who used the skinny little cart system, which brings up an essential point.

The skinny cart worked for Erica, but not me

Even if we can get past the shame of opening the doors of our messy houses or apartments to our organizers or friends, we can't use the systems that work for *them*. We must have systems that are *ours*. Erica knows this by heart; she has tried to help me develop my own set of organization rules. After a fair trial, we took the skinny filing cart out of my kitchen.

Several months later, an ADD acquaintance told me about a revolving plastic organizer that she uses with great success. I bought one, and it worked like a charm. My important papers were corralled and I could always find the unopened mail. That organizer is still in my kitchen today. Of course, I "went overboard" and bought two more for my office. I'm still smiling. And Erica is happy that I have a workable solution.

Label, label strong and able

Probably the single most important thing Erica has introduced to me in the years I've known her is a Brother-brand labeler. My handwriting sucks and I hate printing labels from the computer, so this little machine comes in handy when I need to be able to write something that I (and others) can actually read.

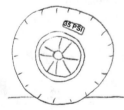

Over the years, I have labeled makeup containers, dog leashes, light switches, baking supplies, door openers, electrical panels, and my favorite: the hubcaps of my car (with the tire inflation pressure limits, which I can never read without a flashlight and a pair of reading glasses).

Labels on tires?

For every brilliant organizing solution that works for me, there are a dozen that I have discarded. It usually takes me several runs at a clutter problem before I settle into a solution that works long term. But I honestly don't mind; problem-solving is one of my favorite pasttimes; it challenges my ADD brain.

Strangely, organizing soothes me. I'm pretty good at it. In fact, Erica tells me she gets her best ideas from me (and then I ask her why I am paying her instead of the other way around!). I seriously considered becoming a professional organizer many years ago. But creating an organizing system and maintaining one require two very different skill sets. I am terrific at the creative side—not so good at the keeping-it-up side.

Creative. That's what Erica calls my filing system. She grimaces and frowns because I don't file alphabetically. I file by topic. Sometimes, the associations in my head are one-of-a-kind. If my brain thinks of life insurance policies and bicycle warranties in the same breath, that's how I'm going to file them. When I return to the folder, I'll be able to find both.

I don't care if my system is weird or illogical or completely off the deep end. I have to have it this way. This is not a choice or a whim. It's not cute. It's a requirement. That's why labels are so important in my household. Although I keep seemingly contradictory subjects in the same folder, if I slap a label on the outside, even Victor can find the life insurance policies.

Don't *touch* my piles

My dear husband has been a trouper about my piles and disorganization. When my ad agency was at full capacity, I would regularly despair over my bulging file cabinets and increasing paper load. Every three or four months, after my employees were gone for the day, I would start pulling folders out of the cabinets and arranging them on the floor so I could rethink their importance and location. It was exhilarating!

After an hour or two, my first wave of energy would subside and I would step back from my task. Now there were huge piles of folders on the floor, on desks, in the break room, and on the conference table. I had only six hours to get them back into the filing cabinets. Suddenly, I was absolutely paralyzed. I didn't know what folder to pick up first. I was drowning; it was time for Victor triage.

When I called my husband, he immediately agreed to come to my office. He recognized my panic and knew just what to do. He arrived with dinner and his medical journals; we had a quick bite to eat, and then he settled back in my chair to read. That's all he did. He knew better than to help me; if he'd touched my piles, I would have gone ballistic. I simply needed someone in the room so I wasn't alone with this gigantic mess.

He was my life preserver; I found out later that ADD experts call his role a "Body Double."

After several hours, he'd go home (his bedtime is always at ten) and I'd stay to finish up the files, now relaxed and confident that I would actually get some sleep before my employees arrived the next morning. By then, I'd have a brand new filing system to teach them. They were usually less enthusiastic than I was about my creative reorganizing.

I constantly update my systems, on the lookout for solutions that allow me to become more efficient, more productive, and better organized. I am quite sure that I spend more time creating the system than I will save, but I carry on anyway.

Think once

The overarching system I use is what I call "Think Once," also known as "Think Once Really Hard and Then Don't Think About It Again." I developed it during my tenure as president and owner of my advertising agency. It was hard work, but at least we could find anything, anywhere in our offices.

"Think Once" means putting much of my life on autopilot. I take a knotty, repetitive problem—for instance, dealing with incoming mail—and I think hard about the needs and sticking points and desired outcome, approaching it from all angles: *What time does the mail arrive? Who gets the mail? Where does it usually land? Where is a convenient place to store it temporarily? When does it need to be opened? What's usually in the mail? What do I need to do with it? Where do I put the pieces that need my immediate attention? Where do I put the unpaid bills? What do I do with invitations or cards?*

"Think Once" really hard and then don't think about it again

It takes me a while to work through all the questions and my solutions to them, but eventually, I devise a system that will allow me to *not think* about the mail. My body knows exactly what to do with it (without thinking) and so does everyone else in the household (because I've labeled the folders!). Not only do I know what to do with the mail, but when I need something important that has arrived by mail, I know exactly where it's stored.

That assumes, of course, that I am following my own system. Sometimes, I need to "Think Once" several times before the system really "takes." I guess that makes it "Think Several Times." My husband knows how my brain worries a problem to within an inch of its life. He tells me (with apologies to the screenwriters of *Butch Cassidy and the Sundance Kid*): "Keep right on thinking, Butch, that's what you're good at!"

My organizing systems are pretty rigid; woe to the person who messes with them. I am crabby and resentful if someone puts the garden clippers in the bin designated for gloves or discards an empty box I was saving to return the seat covers that don't fit my car.

The point of all this is to calm the trivial and routine chaos in my life so that I can deal more effectively with the chaos that I haven't yet tamed. Think Once works only for things that happen again and again. I need to file my bills every month, sometimes every week so I can Think Once. When I am deciding what to fix for dinner, however, I would prefer to be spontaneous. That works fine, too.

While I am a fan of systems like Think Once, I am also aware that no matter how efficient I become, I will continue to misplace vitally important items in my life. That's when I Take Two.

It takes two, baby

I like to have duplicates of things I use often, like reading glasses. Every time I go to my favorite discount store, I buy a couple more pair. There are probably fifteen pairs floating around my house, office and car at any given moment, each with a braided neck cord so I don't lose them.

I have four complete sets of makeup: one for home, one for the car, one for work, and one for travel. Then I never have to show up at a business meeting without mascara (yes, it's happened more than once).

Medication is high on my list of duplicates. I keep a smattering of each of my meds in my purse, my bathroom, the glove compartment, my top desk drawer and even in Victor's car.

I like to keep a generous stash of my favorite pens, too. I stuff them in my purse and in notebooks so I have them at my fingertips. It drives me wild when someone leaves the top off and the ink dries out. Off to the store to buy more of them!

In the kitchen, I have several sets of measuring cups and measuring spoons. I even have three sets of mixing bowls, multiple cookie sheets and five muffin tins. I'll do anything to avoid washing dishes in the middle of cooking—it's distracting!

Now that I've spilled my guts about my organization routine, it sounds like I have a touch of Obsessive Compulsive Disorder

(OCD). Ah, just what I need, another psychological diagnosis with a bunch of initials to remember. But I doubt that it's true OCD. I think it's more ADDiva.

With all the concentrated thought, creative systems, and help from Erica, it seems that I should have my life under control. I only wish that were true. I get busy. Systems fall apart.

I am frustrated because I know that just under the surface, beneath the unkempt clutter and teetering piles, I am pretty well organized. It just looks less than optimal when someone drops by unexpectedly.

Or even when I am expecting them. Inevitably I try to clean out too much clutter before my guests arrive and then have to throw things into a closet or drawers or a room. Then things are in even worse disarray. I'll have to sort them out all over again!

So, while I doubt that I'll ever be a professional organizer, I do think I've earned a similar title. How about "Professional *Dis*-organizer?" Yeah, there's a label an ADD woman could wear with understanding and good humor. Now where did I last use my Brother labeler?

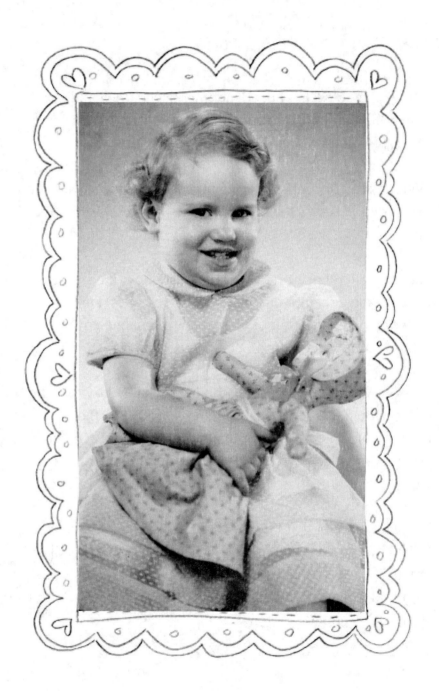

9

The Goldilocks effect

Awwww ... what a sweet picture! I'm two years old, smiling for the camera, head tilted, chin nestled into the collar of my new dress.

Every time I see that picture, I cringe. It's the dress. I can still feel the pale blue, prickly fabric rubbing a raw place around my neck. The crinkly skirt left marks on the backs of my legs and the stiff waistband was torture for my little girl tummy. I don't know how the photographer forced a smile out of me. And I don't know how my mother forced me into that dress.

That dress has affected every single clothing purchase I've made in my grown-up life. Forget style or color; I walk through department stores caressing the fabrics. My wardrobe is full of sweatpants, soft nightgowns, and cushy socks—and thank goodness for stretch jeans!

My primary criterion for clothes is whether they are "forgetta-ble." By me. That's right, I want to wear clothes that fade into the background of my mind so I am not distracted by them. I need clothes that don't require constant supervision—"low-maintenance" clothes, if you will.

I've been tortured by a lot of high-maintenance women's clothes. Anything with a scarf means I spend the day fussing with the knot. Lacy underwear causes repeated (and surrepti-tious) tugs at my crotch. And silk? Don't get me started—a fabric that gets stained by water droplets when I wash my hands *and* needs to be dry cleaned? No thanks. I'll stick with my tagless tees and slacks with a touch of Spandex.

I'm at the mercy of what I call the "Goldilocks Effect"—extraordinary sensitivity that shows up for many of us with ADD. We run from fluorescent light bulbs that hum and flicker. We constantly turn down the TV. We go to networking events, but hide in the bathroom to escape the noise. We eat buttered toast with orange juice, but only when the juice is cold and the toast is warm.

The reason is pretty simple: our brains take in a lot more data from the outside world than we can handle, and we need to close the barn door a bit so we aren't distracted by the small stuff.

We see the BIG PICTURE

and the small picture

π
3.14159265

Attention Deficit Disorder is badly named; there is no lack of attention for ADD women. We pay attention to everything. We see the Big Picture and the Small Picture.

Victor and I once walked into the office of a marriage counselor we had been seeing weekly for several months. I stopped at the doorway, noticing that the entire aura of the room had changed. I identified it in an instant: new carpeting. The therapist was amazed at how quickly I noticed it. Victor was focused on the session and never would have noticed the carpeting without my prompt.

This is one of the true paradoxes of ADD: we overlook important details like decimal points and the street address of our next meeting, yet we sweep trivial data into our brains that others miss: a slightly crooked picture frame, the refrigerator motor, a tiny flaw in the topcoat of our fingernail polish. It all goes back to our ADD prefrontal cortex and how it fails to separate the chaff from the grain.

When Victor walked into the session, his brain could tune out the extraneous input it was receiving. He "saw" the new carpeting, but his brain made an executive decision to ignore it in favor of thinking about the session. More correctly, it was an executive function decision; his prefrontal cortex set priorities that matched the situation.

The sensory input I received was identical to Victor's (same room, same therapist, same desk), but in my head, the facts danced around like little jumping beans. Since my brain function is more in the ranks of middle management than executive, it grabbed the first and strongest impression it received: the "feel" of the room. While there's nothing wrong with admiring new carpeting, it should not have been at the top of the importance heap.

The tipping point

As human beings, we absorb a staggering amount of input through our five senses—words, images, impressions. But as ADD beings, our brains aren't good at sifting through the thousands of bits of data. So it all simmers—minutiae and important stuff together—in a gigantic, information stew. As a result, we are always full to overflowing with miscellaneous tidbits that vie for our erratic attention. As fast as we shuffle a few to the background, a fresh onslaught of data floods our brains. That leads to problems deciding whether to keep the title to the car or to shred it. Decisions are a thorn in the brain for the ADD data stew.

With a mishmash of data simmering in our brains, it doesn't take much to push us over the edge. A ticking clock, a buzzy fly, a flickering fluorescent light bulb; they drive us bananas. Suddenly we ignore the rest of the simmering data and focus on the annoying sound: tick-tick-tick. It's like water torture for us. We run for cover or throw the clock out the window. Our reactions certainly lend more credence to our "selfish" diva status.

But our high level of sensitivity to ticking clocks or noisy flies is not born of high-handed diva snobbery. Our ADD brains are already processing more than they can handle, so we need to limit the external distractions that are within our control. Almost every ADDiva has set up her life to accommodate her particular idiosyncrasies. And there is no consistency among our sensitivites; we each have our very own collection.

Like Goldilocks, some of us must have a bed that is not-too-hard, not-too-soft, but juuuuuust right. Ditto for pillows. And nightgowns.

Some of us are sensitive to light. Flashing strobe lights will push all their ADD brain buttons. Some of us can sleep during the day with the curtains wide open while others wear blindfolds at night to block even the smallest ray of light.

There are ADDivas with strong sensitivity to odor. Perfume or smoke from a wood fire can bring on a

Don't put a pea under an ADDiva's mattress!

headache. My particular trigger is the smell of acrylic finger-nails in beauty salons; I run the other way.

There are ADD women who need the constant noise of the TV or radio; it helps them concentrate. Noise can serve as a "fidget" for the brain. Part of our overactive brains concen-trates on the noise, which frees up the rest of our attention for the task at hand.

But for me, background noise is my enemy, it destroys my concentration, at least when it comes from an outside source, Recently I realized that I was constantly "singing" or playing songs in my head while I worked. The telltale sign was my big toes; I wiggle them inconsciously in time to my internal music. It's like having my own private brain-focus radio station.

For years I have tapped my thumbs on the steering wheel of my car in rhythym to a song I was "playing" in my head. One day I brough the song into my conscious mind and was star-tled to recognize is as the theme song from *Captain Kangaroo*, one of my favorite childhood TV shows!

Midlife women, of course, have the additional joy of tempera-ture sensitivity. This is not caused by ADD, but it sure makes for a gigantic distraction. One minute we're hot, the next we're cold. I can't count the times I put my jacket on and take it off again each day. And, of course, my jacket is a soft cotton knit without tags. It's also one size too big.

One of my hypersensitive issues is fit. I don't like tight clothing—not even skinny jeans. If a garment has plenty of stretch, I'll consider wearing it, but I usually buy clothes that are roomy. Big shoulders, long arms, stretchy waistbands: after years of following fashion trends, I'm content to wear clothes that are less constricting and more forgiving. Now that I think about it, it might not be an ADD issue at all. Maybe it's an over-fifty thing.

The energetic touch

Then there's the issue of touch—not from fabrics or mattresses, but from other people. I'm a natural born hugger, but I've learned to ask permission from other ADD women before I reach out and give them a friendly squeeze. Some of us would rather not be touched and that's OK. We are doing a delicate balancing act within, and unwanted or unexpected physical contact might topple our composure.

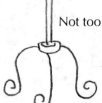

Not too tight, please!

Even I find myself less receptive to touch when I am drowning in the information stew. One day, I love snuggling with Victor; the next day, I can barely stand the weight of his hand on my shoulder. He tries to understand and honor my kinesthetic ebb and flow, but I'm sure it's perplexing.

Many ADD women are highly sensitive to other people's energy, too. We somehow "know" when someone is upset or anxious. We either instinctively back away from high intensity or move toward it, depending on whether we're Inattentive or Hyperactive. We can tell when something is off-kilter with our loved ones before a word is spoken.

I tend to scoop up the energy of the people near me and take it on as my own. For a long time, I was confused that I felt sad or angry for no apparent reason. Then I found out that the energy and emotion originated not from me, but from friends and colleagues who were out of sorts (as if I don't have enough going on in my own brain!). When I recognize the external source, I put up a protective shield so that I can empathize but not drown in their emotion.

There's no empirical evidence to support my hunch that we ADDivas are more intuitive than others, but there is a potentially plausible explanation. Our cognitive skills are unreliable, so perhaps we become more attuned to energy and feelings. It might be a spontaneous ADD compensation; intuition bypasses the vaunted executive function.

For good

Regardless of their particular manifestation, we can use our sensitivities as a force for good in our ADD lives. If we are sensitive to noise, not only can we avoid brass bands, but we can use soothing sounds to calm our frazzled brains. My favorites include the sound of ocean surf and soft meditation music.

Instinctively, I discovered the soothing sounds solution early in my life. When I was nine years old, I saved up my allowance to buy a 99-cent LP of tinkling piano music so I could slow down my brain and drift off to sleep at night. In those days, you were allowed to listen to a record before you bought it. The clerk at Kresge's was quite amused as she played Eddie Duchin for my musical consideration.

My tactile sensitivities lean toward velvety, soft fabrics so I have a collection of plush throws and blankets. When I run my fingers throught the *faux* fur, my mood is much improved.

Escape from the world of sensitivities is warranted sometimes. When I manage to find a quiet, semi-dark room to be alone, I slow down my breathing. The tension slides off my shoulders and I let my brain run at its own pace. Eventually I settle into a less harried mood and my sensitivity antennae can relax.

The world doesn't offer these opportunities without effort; we must find or create them for ourselves. We can add a private moment, a quick nap, or a soothing melody here and there without harm to others and with great benefit to us.

In the meantime, you know where to find me. I'll be in the "soft, loose, and stretchy" clothing department, caressing the fabrics.

The quick brown
fox jumped
over the lazy
dog

10

Totally ineligible...er, illegible

N ormally, I don't pay much attention to the bank receipt after I've deposited money into our account. But as I pulled away from the drive through window, I glanced down at the slip of paper the teller had given me. It reflected a fifteen-hundred dollar deposit.

What? I parked the car and raced into the bank. The check I had deposited was for fifteen *thousand* dollars.

"Oh, is *that* what it was?" the teller asked, with a bemused expression. "I couldn't read your handwriting."

My handwriting. My wretched handwriting. This time, it had nearly cost me $13,000—not to mention the check to the tax office that would have bounced. Red-faced, I left the bank. I was relieved, but once again ashamed of my "sloppy" handwriting.

Recently, I found some of my first-grade papers with primitive A, B, Cs printed between the faint, dotted, blue lines. They looked like the work of any other beginner. But somewhere between block printing and cursive, my handwriting took a nosedive and never recovered.

Today, I combine printing and cursive when I write but it's still illegible. Even Victor does a better job of deciphering the grocery list than I do. Sometimes, though, he calls me from Aisle 3 at Kroger, wondering why we need "paste." It's "pasta," for Pete's sake!

Recently I learned that my poor handwriting stems from … you guessed it: my ADD. There's even a fancy name for it: dysgraphia, a "disorder of written expression" according to the DSM-IV. The definition, in part, is: "writing skills … that fall substantially below those expected, given the individual's chronological age, measured intelligence, and age-appropriate education." Dysgraphia is considered a learning disorder (LD).

How many ways to write illegibly?

ADD and learning disorders tend to hold hands a lot. Adults and children with ADD may have *dyslexia* (difficulty reading, misplacing letters), *dyscalculia* (difficulty with numbers and math), or other learning disorders like *dysgraphia*, which is considered to be strictly a handwriting issue by the International Dylexia Association.

Dr. Ruthmary Deuel, a professor of child neurology at St. Louis University, has identified three subtypes of dysgraphia: motor dysgraphia, spatial dysgraphia, and dyslexic dysgraphia. Lucky us! We can have one, two or three of the subtypes in any combination.

— **Motor dysgraphia** presents with handwriting that is virtually illegible, although the spelling is usually OK. With extreme effort, people with motor dysgraphia can write short paragraphs with some legibility—but on longer writing samples, their handwriting deteriorates.

Folks with motor dysgraphia also have below normal "finger-tapping speed," which measures keyboarding skills, as in computers or typewriters.

My strong suspicion is that I would qualify for a diagnosis of motor dysgraphia. My handwriting has always been a mess. Even if I slow down to a turtle's pace (which makes me anxious and impatient), I can barely eke out a few legible lines before I revert to "messy." And my typing speed

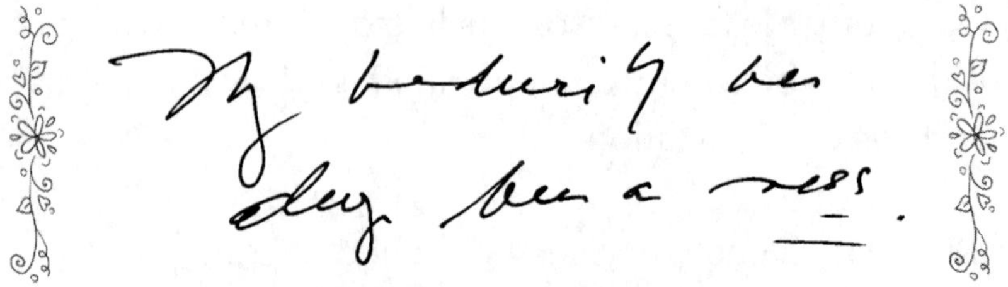

[handwritten text]

never improved much more than forty-five words per minute despite working on typewriters and computers my entire professional life!

— **Spatial dysgraphia**, as the name implies, is difficulty with estimating the amount of space allotted for handwriting. I may snuggle into this diagnosis, too. My hand-addressed envelopes inevitably have letters squished together on the far right side where I miscalculated space. And I waste more than my share of those cute little notecards when I run out of room at the bottom.

I do rewrite them so the spacing will be better, but my fingers and brain fatigue so quickly that my last effort is usually worse than my first. Sometimes, I revert to email. Or, sorry to say, I don't send a thank-you note at all.

— **Dyslexic dysgraphia**. People with this subtype have unusual (or creative) spelling and illegible handwriting. If the person with this subtype copies from another written document, their handwriting improves, which is not true with the other subtypes. In an interesting paradox, a person can have dyslexic dysgraphia without having true dyslexia.

Though I doubt that I have dyslexic dysgraphia, my spelling has deteriorated with age. I once prided myself on being able to ignore spell check on my computer. Now I find myself writing "got" instead of "god." *(True confessions time: when I proofread this paragraph, I realized I had mixed up the letters in the word "dyslexic" as "dsylexic" and typed the word "spelling" as "speeling." Maybe I do have dyslexic dysgraphia!)*

Da ADD bone connected to da dysgraphia bone ...

There is a distinct correlation between ADD and dysgraphia, according to research conducted within the last ten years. Folks with ADD have trouble with visual-spatial relationships. That's noticing and drawing conclusions from the location of one object in relation to another one. Visual-spatial problems crop up in reading, math, and handwriting, all of which can be troublesome for the ADD population.

Reading is a challenge for many of the ADD women I meet. They tell me it was torture to plow through academic textbooks with a lot of dark print and boring content. I can empathize; sometimes I would read the same paragraph three or four times before I realized I had no idea what it meant. My solution was to read the material out loud until I "caught" the drift. Then I could read normally.

Algebra is another ADD nightmare. Fortunately for me, my dad helped me every night at the kitchen table. He must have done a good job, because I placed into advanced math classes in high school. But it wasn't a natural ability; at the first opportunity, I opted out of college math. It's one of the reasons I sidestepped medical school, which had been one of my childhood dreams.

A 2007 study showed that ADD students often reverse, omit or add letters to words when they write. Check! I constantly leave off the last letters of words. "Agony" becomes "ago" and "together" becomes "toga"—quite different words with quite different meanings.

I am very sensitive about my handwriting. There is something shameful about my inability to master something so basic. So as much as possible, I try to avoid sending handwritten letters.

My friends save the postcards I send them from vacation (I try to print neatly). They have so much trouble translating the words, they jokingly tell me my postcards take on new meaning every time they read them. *Very funny.*

A few years ago, I was writing a check for groceries under the watchful eye of the cashier. When I handed her the check, she squinted at it, then gave it back to me. "What *is that* number?" she said contemptuously. "You'll have to write another check. The bank won't take it if they can't read it." I wanted to fall through the floor. With five people in line behind me witnessing the entire humiliation, I wrote out another check and

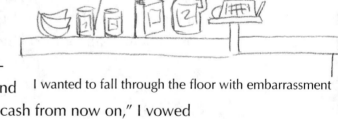

I wanted to fall through the floor with embarrassment

grabbed my groceries. "I'll carry cash from now on," I vowed grimly as I escaped the store.

Technology to the rescue!

The electronic age has rescued me from most of my dysgraphic shame. I rarely write checks anymore, thanks to online banking. When my youngest son needs an infusion of cash, I can send it to him on the internet.

Even my grocery list is printed from my computer and posted on my refrigerator; I just check off the items we need. And now when I pay for my groceries, I merely slide my debit card through the little machine, punch in my numbers (slowly—remember, my "tapping speed" is below normal) and poof! I'm out the door. Take that, rude and inconsiderate cashier!

I have no excuse for not sending thank-you cards these days. I navigate over to the online greeting card website, choose a card, and type a personal message (they offered a custom font created from my handwriting, but I declined). Then the company prints it, sticks it in an envelope, stamps it, and mails it for me. It's an ADD dream come true! Now my friends know how grateful I am for their kindnesses.

In the past, I've scribbled phone numbers so quickly that I couldn't read them—or I left off the last digit, which renders the entire number useless. Now I ask people to send me an email or text message with an important phone number. Then I can automatically transfer it to my electronic address book without writing (or typing) it myself.

Technology may be pushing handwriting into obsolescence. In California, students are taught handwriting in third and fourth grades, but by the fifth grade, they switch to the computer.

From then on, they compose and format their schoolwork in a word processing program.

There has been a cry of outrage from penmanship purists, who lament the loss of handwritten correspondence. I understand their anger; I have a treasure chest full of love letters that are deeply intimate instead of electronically sound.

Love letters should
be handwritten.
Or not.

While the handwriting advocates wail, however, my ADD shouts with delight. It is delectable to have come of age in a time where my illegible handwriting has become (mostly) a non-issue. Three cheers for email, word processing, and the typed word!

11

It's about time

You're always such a *presence* when you come into a room," the man on my publicity committee confided, with obvious admiration. I was flattered until he added: "You're always so *windblown*!"

"Windblown," indeed. What I was, was late.

I hate being late more than anything in the world. I hate hurrying. I hate the embarrassment of disturbing the rest of the crowd. I hate the raised eyebrows and the irritated sighs. I just hate being late.

So why am I late to almost everything, everywhere? For reasons that are murky even to the most brilliant scientists, ADD brains have trouble with time. We can judge the passage of time as well as anyone else, but when we apply it to tasks, we miss the mark.

Like many of my ADD sisters, I dislike time constraints. I feel pushed around by them. Alarm clocks, deadlines, appointments—they're like iron fences around my precious life. I really want my time to be my own. After all, isn't that all we really have in life—time? I suspect my tardiness might be infused with a hint of rebellion.

But there have been occasions when I tersely watch the clock and steel myself to be prompt. Since the passage of time is so mysterious to me, there is a good chance that I will bump into the opposite side of the time continuum: I will arrive too early. And then I will have to wait. I hate waiting almost as much as I hate being late.

I try to be patient. I am not patient. I hum, I pace, I wiggle. The obvious solution would be to take along something to do, like a book or my planner. But if I took time to find something to do on the chance that I would be early, I would end up being...late!

Miscalculating time has been such a persistent issue for me that I have given it considerable thought (accompanied by steady stream of self-recrimination). I've come up with four major reasons I am late, all of them straight from the ADD Playbook.

1. Underestimate? Who, me?

First, I am supremely confident that I can get ready in half the time it actually takes. I'm not sure where this optimistic attitude originated, but it's certainly not based in reality. I check the clock and convince myself that there is ample time to shower, dress, apply makeup, gather my papers, find my purse, keys, and shoes (they are always hiding), and get in the car (for the final time) in twenty minutes flat. *Never gonna happen.*

This all-too-common ADD misconception has its roots in our flawed executive function, that process that takes place in the prefrontal cortex. If you recall, our dear ADD friend, Ms. Prefrontal Cortex, has a tendency to take long coffee breaks. Without her guidance, we find it tough to accurately estimate the amount of time it will take to get to an important (or even an unimportant) appointment.

Time estimation requires planning and working memory. It involves that complicated balance between thinking ahead to what is supposed to happen in the future and being present in the moment to handle in-this-moment events. Working memory allows us to remember both sets of information in our minds at once and then rearrange the data to produce a desired action.

There are several kinds of memory, as catalogued by psychologists. Long-term memory allows those of us "of a certain age" to remember all the words to "She Loves You" (yeah, yeah, yeah). Short-term memory means we hear the wind chimes, but they have no bearing on our task, so their echo fades from conscious thought.

Working memory takes short-term memories and extends their half-life until they are used, and then discards them. But Ms. Prefrontal Cortex and her working memory partners—the brain's parietal cortex, basal ganglia, and anterior cingulate (located throughout our marvelous brains)—can't quite overcome the ADD breakdowns in our neurological network.

When I try to estimate the amount of time it takes me to get out the door, my working memory isn't living up to its full potential. Distractions arise, my working memory can't compete with my fascination for the distraction—and I end up being late.

Surely there must have been a day in my life when the stars aligned, the angels sang, and I actually did get out the door in twenty minutes—or I thought I did. I might have read the digital clock backwards (from the shower, I can only catch a glimpse of it in the mirror). Or I actually might have started earlier; sometimes it's hard to remember the exact moment that I shift into high gear.

I truly want to believe in the mythical twenty-minute departure, in much the same way I want to believe in Tinkerbell and Glinda the Good Witch. Fairy tales do come true, don't they? Yes, but only if I manage to tear myself away from whatever I'm doing. Which brings me to Reason Number Two that I'm late: transitions.

I believe, I believe!

2. Transitions, torment my heart; transitions, keep us apart

When I am finally able to focus on something, I don't want to stop. I'm "in the zone," productive at last! I have marshaled my cerebral resources toward one shining, glorious goal. I can see the next step and the one that follows it. The end is in sight. I know that, if I stop working, I may never be able to muster this kind of concentration again.

Sometimes, I am so intent on my task that I am oblivious to hunger, thirst, fatigue—even bathroom breaks (until the last, urgent moment). I've been known to sit down at the computer for a few moments and, by the time I look at the clock again,

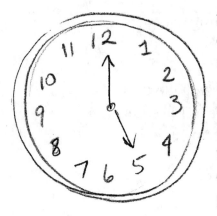

three hours have melted away. That's irrelevant when I have a long stretch of time, but not when my calendar repeatedly calls to me: "Your appointment begins in forty-five minutes." "Your appointment begins in thirty minutes." "Your appointment will begin in five minutes." I know I should be slowing down, circling the paperwork wagons, and putting away my Number Two pencils.

But I don't want to tidy up, either. If I stash all that stuff, I'll just have to get it out again when I come back to my desk. So why put it away in the first place? It will save me time later and it will buy me a few more minutes of focused work right now. So I work a little longer—a little longer than I anticipated, that is. And then, I am late again. Darn it.

But there are other transition troubles that have nothing to do with hyperfocus. ADD folks have difficulty moving from one task to another, like transitioning from wakefulness to sleep.

Winken, Blynken, and the Anti-Nod

At ten o'clock, Victor gives me a kiss and heads for bed, every single night of his life. "I'll be right there," I say. He nods and smiles, knowing full well that it could be thirty minutes or five hours before I snuggle up next to him.

Many nights, I am sleepy at 7 p.m., but by nine, I get my second wind. My brain wakes up, ready to boogie. Rather than transitioning into sleep, I am fired up. I want to watch the end of a TV show or write a blog post or answer one more email. My most productive work hours are from 11 p.m. to 4 a.m.

I'm sure it's because there are fewer distractions. It's dark outside, so I can't see the garden or birds. The dogs are sleeping. No phone calls come in. I can focus.

[I have another theory as to why I stay up late at night, although it is completely unproven. I was born at 11 p.m., so my first hours alive were in the wee hours of the morning. Perhaps my circadian rhythm was set on that fateful April evening. Then again, it could be my ADD brain!]

Sleep and the ADD brain make a comical pair. Most of the ADD people I know stay up late. Some of us go to bed at a reasonable hour yet can't fall asleep. With the lights turned off and no visual distractions, we are alone with our racing thoughts and wild imaginations. We try deep breathing, relaxation, or a warm bath, but only when our minds ease their frenetic pace do we slumber.

Some of us get to sleep but wake up a few hours later. And a smattering of ADD folks love sleeping so much we'd stay in bed twenty-two hours a day if given half a chance!

Studies show that even people without ADD exhibit ADD-ish symptoms so true-blue ADD folks with a sleep deficit get a double dose of their favorites: inattention, impulsivity and dis-tractibility. And distractions make me late far too often.

3. A little flitting before leaving

Flitting is fun!

There is a direct correlation between the number of minutes I have allotted to prepare for departure and the number of distractions that will co-opt those minutes. The more minutes I have, the more susceptible I am to butterfly flitting.

With plenty of time ahead of me, I indulge in the luxury of tak-ing a few pictures of the redbud trees in bloom and transfer-ring them to my computer. Then I notice that the color is a bit washed out, so I open the photo adjustment program and start to work. In the process, I discover the pictures from my husband's birthday party that need a little work, too, but —*oops! I must get ready!*

I pull out my briefcase and gather the files I will need for the meeting but they aren't in the correct color sequence. So I go to the storage closet to get some new folders and the labeler; my client will be impressed that I am so organized! There are even more files in the wrong color folders in my cabinet so I start to work on them but—*Oh, look at the time! I must get ready!*

I resolutely march into the hall to get my coat and gloves, load the files into my car, and look for my purse and keys. Fortunately, I have a beeper on both of them, so if I can find my purse, I can locate the keys by "ringing" the beeper. The keys are next to the mail, so I take a minute to flip through the envelopes; there might be something I need for this meeting. *Yikes! If I don't leave now, I'll be late!* Butterfly flitting has eaten up all those lovely, spare minutes.

Which comes first, the chicken or the egg?

A close relative of butterfly flitting is the Priority Plague. A well-known time management expert, Stephen Covey, suggests we use a quadrant system to set priorities. His four quadrants are: Urgent and Important (getting to the hospital when you're in labor), Urgent but Unimportant (a sale on surfboards that ends at midnight when you don't surf), Important but Non-Urgent (the tax deadline is six months from now) and Unimportant and Non-urgent (replacing the kitchen sink when the old one is in perfect condition).

ADD brains don't discriminate about information they process, so it's tough to figure out which quadrant applies to any particular event or task. *Everything* is a top priority for ADD brains, which is the same as saying there are no priorities at all.

It's like a world in which everyone measures seventy-two inches from head to toe; there is no "tall" or "short," there is only one size. For us, all our tasks are seventy-two inches tall. And because people "out there" get crazy excited about getting things done, we decide that *all* our tasks must be really, really important and really, really urgent.

When I get ready for an appointment or a movie or a lunch date or a phone call, I see a lot of Important and Urgent tasks that should be completed before the Important and Urgent appointment or movie or lunch date or phone call. I try to squeeze in "one more thing" before I run to the bus stop. I try hard to please everyone and, in the process, I please no one—especially myself.

It's enough to make me want to go on a sit-down strike. And sometimes I do, which is Reason Number Four that I am late: procrastination.

4. I'll do it tomorrow

Procrastination is the fine art of doing tomorrow what should have been done yesterday, and I am its most ardent devotee. I can conjure credible delays for virtually any situation. "It's too muggy outside." "I have writer's block." "I need to wash the car." I have actually completed tasks on which I had previously procrastinated, in order to procrastinate on other tasks.

I procrastinate with reluctance, of course. I don't want an ever larger backlog of items on my To Do list. But procrastination can be a potent form of self-medication for ADD. The adrenaline rush is akin to taking prescription stimulant medication.

When we absolutely, positively cannot procrastinate another minute, we rush around, drive over the speed limit, and screech into our seats in the back row. That's pretty thrilling stuff; it wakes up our brains so we can focus and get moving.

I'm not a risk-taker; in fact, my husband calls me "risk averse." But I push my adrenaline levels sky high when I set up tight deadlines and then scamper hastily to meet them.

My "risky business" isn't sky-diving or race car driving—it's procrastination and running late. They're effective, but they're also rough on my poor adrenal glands. I've had so many deadline-driven occupations that I have fried my adrenaline system to a crisp.

Sometimes, procrastination and perfectionism skip along together in an "evil twins" sort of plot. I have set impossibly high standards for myself and then procrastinated because I couldn't meet them. When I am finally forced to churn out some kind of finished product, it is vastly inferior to my own expectations. That gives me an opportunity to offer a fabulous and plausible excuse: "If I'd only had more time, I could have done a better job." Since I am the one who "wasted" her time, the excuse is a tad self-serving.

Years of procrastination and slap-dash results made me wonder if I really was capable of doing a better job, even if I had an infinite amount of time. Perhaps the only way I can finish *anything* is to procrastinate—and then finish in the nick of time.

And we *do* finish things. We accomplish an amazing amount of work in a compressed amount of time. Therein lies the rub for ADD folks like us: procrastination works. We not only get the thrill of the last-minute chase, but we enjoy the thrill of successful completion, even when we should have fallen on our little ADD faces.

Without exception, those of us in ADD Land who procrastinate have had at least one procrastination blow-up in our pasts. The fall-out from that catastrophe should have taught us never to procrastinate again. But we forget and do it anyway—which is exactly what happened when Victor and I were on the way to Spain.

Procrastination luck runs out

One of the perks of Victor's job is that he has the opportunity to travel to conferences around the world. Lucky me, I get to tag along sometimes. Several years ago, he was a speaker at a conference in Madrid, Spain. We had reserved our airline seats months in advance and planned our hotel and itinerary. It was the evening of our departure.

As usual, my Covey quadrants were a bit off-kilter, as was my working memory. I had procrastinated all day and was packing my last pair of shoes. Victor was getting a little antsy; we needed to be on the way to the airport by now. But I wasn't worried. I blithely continued packing and flitting and underestimating as the minutes ticked by.

At ninety minutes before flight time (when we should have been checked in for an overseas flight) we got in the car and I burned rubber toward the expressway. I had calculated exactly how long it would take to get there. It was Friday night; the lines would be long, but there would be more agents on duty, too. We'd make it just fine.

But that was the night my procrastination streak of luck ran out. There had been a wreck on I-40 and traffic was backed up for miles. Heart pounding, I took the first possible exit so that I could detour around the gridlock. Everyone else had the same idea, so Highway 70 was equally clogged. I began to panic. Victor didn't say a word, but I sensed his disgust and anger.

At thirty minutes before flight time, I was almost in tears; I was furious with myself. I finally pulled off the road and called the airline, explained that we were caught in a traffic jam (which was the truth, but only part of the reason we were late). The ticket agent had been fielding similar calls for hours; the traffic had delayed many other passengers. She patiently explained that we'd need to come to the airport to exchange our tickets for a later flight.

The silence in the car was heavy and dull. I screamed at myself for being stupid and slow and why did Victor love me and he's gonna divorce me and maybe I needed to stay home and let him go alone and this was the last time I would ever procrastinate. All that went on inside my body. Out-side, I gripped the steering wheel and headed for the airport. I felt wretched.

We made the ticket exchange—there was a flight at 11 a.m. the next day—and I started the horrible drive back to our house. About twenty minutes from home, Victor turned to me and said, "We have an entire evening to ourselves. Let's do something fun together!"

I stared at him. Was he kidding? I had cost us an entire day in Spain and now he was suggesting that we have fun in North Carolina?

"But I … I made us late," I said, voice cracking. "You must hate me."

"I can't possibly beat you up as badly as you beat yourself up," he said gently. "You do a great job of it. But what's done is done. We are going to Madrid in the morning. We're safe. My presentation isn't affected. So let's go out to dinner and have an evening to ourselves."

I cried. I didn't deserve this man, that's for sure. He meant it. No harsh words, no humiliation, no guilt. He *meant* it.

Yes, I was late—seriously late. I had screwed up and couldn't pull the rabbit out of the hat at the last minute. My ADD had been in full bloom but that didn't excuse my actions. Instead of blame, Victor chose forgiveness, understanding and cooperation. We were OK; that was all that mattered.

And we arrived two hours early for the flight the next morning.

Procrastination is the
fine art of doing
tomorrow what
should have been done
yesterday

"A friend is one to whom
one may pour out
the contents of one's heart,
chaff and grain together,
knowing that the gentlest of hands
will take it and sift it,
keep what's worth keeping
and blow the rest away."

--Dinah Craik

adapted from *A Life for a Life* 1859

12

The Secret

For my tenth birthday, I had a big party and invited my class-mates from school. After refreshments and gifts, we headed down to the creek to catch some tadpoles. I went back to the house to get milk cartons for the tadpoles, and as I returned, I overheard one of the girls say: "Yeah, I didn't want to come, either. I only wanted the ice cream and cake."

I froze, stricken with heartache and sadness. I was an outsider, even at my own party. No one liked *me*; I was the pesky means to an end that apparently was worth a few hours of pretend party spirit. I couldn't say my goodbyes quickly enough. I wanted to run to my room, slam the door, and cry (because it *was* my party and I *could* cry if I wanted to!).

"The Secret" had raised its ugly head once again. I'd always known there was something different about me, something shapeless and terrible that was glaringly obvious to people "out there" but mad-deningly invisible to me. It was as if everyone else had been given

the decoder ring to a happy life while I was stuck with an empty box of Cracker Jacks.

I tried to figure it out, to act like the people I was so desperate to please. I became a consummate people-watcher. I surreptitiously studied the mannerisms of the popular girls, then went home to try them myself while watching myself in the mirror. The new affectations didn't help my popularity.

So I implemented a vigorous self-improvement program. After my mother tucked me in at night, I stayed awake rehearsing hypothetical dialogues in my head. If I made a social *faux pas* during this imaginary conversation, I would start again, practicing until I had mastered (what I hoped were) the correct words for a happy ending.

Perhaps if I wore the right clothes, I thought, my social status would improve. I devoured teen fashion magazines to see how the really cool girls dressed. One fall, my mom and I drove ninety miles to St. Louis to buy a black-and-white-checked, wool skirt and vest that had been featured on the cover of *Seventeen* magazine—only to discover that it looked far less appealing on me than it had on the Twiggy-like models.

But The Secret wasn't about the clothes I wore or the manner-isms I tried to mimic ; it was personal. It was about *me*. And though I didn't know it then, it was about my ADD.

I had no idea that my loud, brash voice was the result of my uninhibited prefrontal cortex. I would never have believed that girls in my class were turned off by my bossiness, an external compensation for my brain's lack of internal control. I was told repeatedly that I was "too intense," which I now know was a byproduct of my ADD hyperfocus.

Without diagnosis, without treatment, without resources, I grabbed the best, most viable solution I could think of in the moment: I went into hiding. I would push The Secret under-ground so no one would notice her flaws. But I still had no idea which part of me contained the no-good, very-bad Secret, so I had no choice but to squelch all of the Real Linda. In her place, I installed the facade of a New Linda.

The New Linda emerged just in time. Though we of the flower-child generation were labeled "rebels," like all teen-agers, we were driven to conformity by peer pressure. We parted our long straight hair down the middle, wore our headbands, and dragged our extra-wide bell bottoms on the ground so they frayed enough to reveal our Birkenstock

sandals. At least, many of us chose that lifestyle. Others, like me, took a more conservative tack.

It was hard enough for me to hold the New Linda together without shaking the foundations of society at the same time. While I empathized with the peace movement (and marched in a couple of demonstrations), by the time I got to college, I wanted to join a sorority, the ultimate act of conformity. The New Linda pledged a sorority on M.A.C. Avenue.

There was still a cold little pebble of fear that bounced in my stomach when I thought my Secret might be exposed again. I was hyper-vigilant, looking for subtle signals that I might have crossed the line into social ineptitude: a raised eyebrow, a small sigh, a slight move away from me. I twisted myself into a pretzel to maintain the New Linda facade, a balancing act that required a powerful ally: "The Monitor."

The Monitor has entered my brain

There wasn't a precise day that "The Monitor" took control of my thoughts and actions. It was an insidious conquest, advancing and gaining power as I matured and built a life as the New Linda. It was so well-integrated into my brain that I probably never would have noticed it except for a wise executive coach who worked with me during my ad agency days.

In my early forties, my agency was well-established, but I needed some help with employees and productivity. So I hired Cindy. During one of our coaching sessions, she invited me to try an exercise called "Watching the Mind." She explained that each of us has an internal voice that was once a necessary protector. ("Look both ways before you cross the street!")

As adults, that nagging voice either recedes into the background when we take responsibility for ourselves, or it grows louder and stronger if we mistrust our innate ability to respond appropriately to life's challenges.

It's tricky, this mind monitor of ours. It slips in between our normal brain chatter to insert negative, fearful ideas topped off with a lot of judgment:

> "Don't touch the vase; you'll break it! Remember how clumsy you are?"
> "You interrupt too much! Wait your turn to talk. Wait. Wait. Now you can say something."

"You shouldn't be on that committee; you'll just disappoint everyone like you did last time."

My mind mixed a grain of truth (yes, I disappointed people on the committee) with a pack of lies (the past is not necessarily a prologue to the future, and I might be a great committee member this time). Cindy asked me to pay attention to my mind, listening to the messages as if someone else were speaking to me.

At first, it was hard to separate the mind's directives from my brain chatter—but when I did, I was shocked at its pervasive and strident tone. Not only did my mind boss me around a lot, but it also watched me all the time, on the lookout for a snafu in my behavior or words. It monitored my every move, thus my nickname for it: "The Monitor."

It was easy to see that the Monitor had become the keeper of the New Linda facade (which by now had become simply "Linda"). It was the voice that cautioned me against trusting people with my deepest feelings; it kept me safe by keeping me separate.

If, in some momentary lapse, the door to my Authentic Self opened slightly the Monitor jumped in to snap it shut again, keeping The Secret hidden from public view. The All Powerful

Monitor was much like its distant relative—the All-Powerful Oz. The Monitor hid my true identity behind a thick curtain. And like Oz, the Monitor was a master of disguise; she had masks for every occasion.

The many masks of ADD

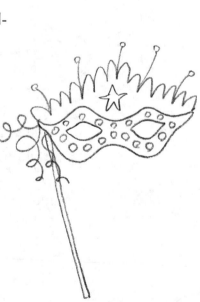

Among the Monitor's collection was the "Intellect" mask. It supplemented my facade when I was in the company of professionals, chamber of commerce types, and really smart folks. It was one of my favorites, since it encouraged me to dazzle people with my intelligence and surprise them with my creative ideas. I relied on the Intellect mask when my social skills failed me.

Another popular choice was the "Perfectionist" mask, which pushed me to work harder, longer, and better than anyone else. This mask earned the nickname "Overcompensation" since it was designed to offset my ADD deficiencies. A variation on the Perfectionist mask was the "Witch" mask (spelled with a "B").

Sometimes, the Monitor chose a mask labeled "The Life of the Party" to ensure that people were laughing with me instead of laughing at me. The Life of the Party mask was much like the clown who laughed on the outside but cried on the inside. Emotional pain is less harmful when it can be deflected.

A disguise that took only minor enhancement from the Monitor was the "Rebel" mask. I was already "different," but this mask allowed me to choose how I would be different. At the extreme, this mask might even be called "Oppositional Defiant Disorder."

A couple of masks the Monitor pulled out in extreme circumstances were "Space Cadet" and "Loser." Both allowed me to linger on the sidelines instead of plowing into the success lane. I could be a ditz, lower my expectations (and the expectations of those near me), and throw myself a massive pity party ("I'll never get it right, so why bother making any effort?").

Over time, the masquerade grew so powerful that the Real Linda was pushed into the recesses of obscurity, but she was never happy about it. Occasionally, she would stamp her foot, demanding to come out and play. She was tired of her tiny, boxed-in home. But the Monitor fought to retain control; it remembered how wildly inappropriate the Real Linda had been in the past.

When I became an adult who was older and somewhat wiser, I listened more intently to the Real Linda. I knew that she was worth liberating from the iron fist of the Monitor. She was the only route to living my life's purpose. So I set out to do battle with the All Powerful Monitor.

I arm wrestled the Monitor into submission by beating her at her own game: I monitored the Monitor. I paid close attention to the voice that ordered me here and there, that gave me play-by-play directions when I interacted with others. At first, I was a dispassionate observer. Later, I interceded on behalf of the Real Linda.

When the Monitor sent down orders, I held the directive on a figurative platter in front of me and then consciously made a choice about whether to accept it. Each time I allowed my authentic self to participate in the choice, the power of the Monitor diminished.

Eventually, the Monitor lost its power over me. It stopped monitoring my behavior. I was perfectly capable of handling my own life and decisions, even with my ADD in play.

If I could time-travel back to that birthday party so many years ago, I'd still have ice cream and cake and we'd collect tadpoles. But I'd invite girls who were funny, creative, and free-spirited. I'd welcome friends who refused a mask of conformity and let themselves out to play every day. I'd invite girls who boosted my confidence instead of shattering it. I'd invite girls *like me*!

That's precisely how I choose my friends today. Life is too short to tolerate toxic, judgmental people. I have people in my life—with ADD or not—who share my joy at being alive. I have people who love me for being the Real Linda. And I love people who are sensitive, sophisticated, simple, loving, warm, wise and wonderful. We bring out the best in each other. That's what friends are all about.

13

Married with ADD

We were ten minutes from the airport when Victor turned to me, puzzled. "You know, I never did get a confirmation of my ticket. You did buy me one, didn't you?"

We were late. Very late. I was driving 74 miles per hour, nine over the speed limit. I had pushed the envelope as far as was practical; if I'd been driving ten over, a speeding ticket might have cost me my license. I didn't let up on the gas.

"I thought your *secretary* got your ticket!" I said, almost exploding.

Crisis arises. I called my assistant and asked her to go online to see if there were any flights to Chicago on the same airline that afternoon. She called me back a few minutes later; there was one seat on a flight that departed one hour after mine. Whew. Crisis averted. The price? $500 for his ticket versus $142 for mine.

I drilled on, flying past exits and onto the airport parkway. Then I slowed down. The speed limit was twenty-five. I throttled the car back to a crawl and finally made it to the parking deck, only to find there were no parking spaces.

Victor, a seasoned traveler, knew this could spell disaster. He was not happy. I was not happy. Finally, on the top level, I found an open spot and we started our dash for the terminal. Maybe we could still make my flight.

The airline is strict about checking luggage; none is accepted within thirty minutes of flight time. I checked in at precisely twenty-nine minutes before flight time, one minute past the cutoff. Second crisis arises. I could fly to Chicago, but *my luggage* could not—and the airlines refused to send my luggage alone. It had to match up to a ticketed passenger on the flight.

I agonized for one precious minute, then came up with a solution. The luggage could fly with Victor on the later flight! But between us, we had four pieces of luggage to check, including lots of equipment for a presentation. The luggage fees would be $25 each for the first and second suitcase, and $100 for each one after that. Second crisis averted. The price? $300.

I kissed Victor goodbye, ran through security, and boarded the plane. I checked in at our hotel and waited to hear from Victor. The wind was fierce in Chicago, but I didn't worry about it until I got a call from Victor. His flight had been delayed due to windy conditions in the Windy City. Crisis Number Three arises.

He called with regular updates but I could tell from the tone of his voice that he was frustrated and tired. The day had been nerve-wracking and I was close to a meltdown, shored up by a nasty dose of guilt and horror at the error of my ADD ways. Five hours later, I picked up my exhausted husband and all four suitcases from the baggage claim area. Crisis Number Three averted. The price? I wasn't sure how much damage had been done to our marriage.

We headed back to the hotel to get a few hours of sleep before the conference started. This would be the first time that we had presented as a couple. The all-too-ironic title of our presentation? "Sailing the Seven Cs to a Great ADHD Relationship."

My husband, my adoring and adorable husband, woke up the next morning, gave me a hug, and said: "I love you. Let's go give them a great presentation." No recrimination. No silent treatment. He lives with my ADD crises every day. He knows the price (in this case, $800). And he loves me anyway.

"It's just a plane ticket" he said. "And we made it. Case closed." It's such a relief to live with someone who forgives me so easily. But, then, Victor does have his *own* peculiarities.

Opposites attract

My husband is a neat-nik, almost to the point of obsession. He tidies his paperwork so it is parallel to the edge of his desk. The papers are stacked from smallest to largest, each positioned in the exact center of the pile, like a small pyramid. He lines up his shaving cream, toothpaste and hair dryer on the bathroom vanity in precisely the same location every morning. Sometimes, I have the insane urge to mess up his papers or move the toothpaste a few inches—but I don't.

Out in the garden, Victor loves to pick blueberries. Well, maybe it's not the picking that he loves; he lives to count things. And he counts every single blueberry that goes into the basket. He'll come into the kitchen with the blueberries, triumphantly announcing, "One thousand, three hundred and forty-four today! That makes three thousand, eight hundred and twenty-one from that bush!" I roll my eyes and make blueberry cobbler.

We are the perfect example of "Opposites Attract," but it hasn't always been a perfect fit. We struggled for years to find our balance. Marriage counseling, individual therapy, couples retreats—we tried almost everything to make it work. And we almost failed, more than once.

In the heat of misunderstanding and miscommunication, we blamed each other for everything that went wrong. "If only he were less rigid, things would be fine." "If only she'd clean up the house, at least we could eat dinner together at the kitchen table!" There were weeks of prideful silence (we were both born under the sign of Taurus, the bull—very stubborn). There were pledges to do better. There were slips and slides and anger and pain.

Our saving grace was the most basic of relationship requirements: commitment. No matter how late I am leaving for the airport or how many blueberries Victor counts, we are committed to stay together. Always. Even when we don't like each other and we wonder why we ever got married in the first place. Even when we want to pull out the old blame game.

We learned a simple phrase that makes all the difference: "We're on the same team." When something goes wrong, we look for solutions together, as we did on that harried Chicago trip. Yes, in this case it was my ADD that screwed up the flight, but the remedy was a mutual effort.

I'm quite sure that my clutter piles and distractibility are difficult for a man who likes his life well-ordered. Amazingly, however, as long as he has his little corner of calm, he can tolerate the chaos of my ADD, which dominates the rest of the corners in our married life. He can actually work by putting his very tidy piles *on top* of my messy piles.

It's almost as if he can block out the mess and focus only on his work. Clearly, he does not have ADD. In the same situation, my ADD brain would see all the piles, be distracted by the messy papers underneath, and have to clean the desk before I started work!

Immediately after I was diagnosed, Victor got a crash course in ADD. He read pertinent sections of *Driven to Distraction* and

> *"...unless you're inside an ADD brain,
> it's hard to fathom how much
> it dominates your life. "*

then decided it would be helpful to point out my ADD actions.
"Uh-oh, there goes your ADD again!" he would say. That was
not a popular decision with me. It took about forty-eight hours
for him to learn to keep his observations to himself.

He tried to understand, heaven knows. But unless you're inside
an ADD brain, it's hard to fathom how much it dominates your
life. The turning point in his ADD education occurred when
he attended a conference specifically for adults with ADD. He
finally "got it" that ADD was about my brain and not about
him. It wasn't personal; I wasn't trying to drive him crazy with
my messy kitchen. It was my brain that kept me from being a
neat-nik like him. He's been supportive ever since.

It's not easy, but it's possible

I know couples who aren't so lucky. He wants the house neat
and clean but she can't keep the clutter at bay. She's always
on time; her partner is fashionably late. Accusations and anger
breed like rabbits, and resentment becomes the order *du jour*.
It's a formula for disaster unless both of the partners are willing

to look honestly at their part in the relationship breakdowns. Then, by learning and applying workable relationships tools, they can transform their lives together—as we did. It was a process that took years for us.

If we can come back from the brink of divorce (as a bitter reminder, I still have the letter he wrote advising me to communicate only through his lawyer), then every ADD couple can do the same. It goes back to Job One: commitment.

I consider Victor something of a saint for living with me. But he considers me a bright light who brings creativity and spontaneity to his life. He doesn't love me *in spite of* my ADD; my ADD is one of the things he loves *about* me. He is in awe of my energy, my enthusiasm and my passion. It's contagious; now he walks with a lilt in his step and a (usually awful) joke in the conversation. I love waking up in the morning to a smile; it starts my day off beautifully. We have a mutual admiration society, and we keep it that way by emphasizing the positives in our relationship every single day.

Friends of mine swoon when they hear about Victor's courageous response to my ADD. They notice how we lovingly look at each other and they want that devotion, too. "Does he have a brother?" they ask, as if the answer to happiness could be found in his family gene pool. (The answer is, "Yes, he has a brother who is happily married, too.")

Our delicious relationship wasn't handed down through our respective histories. Our families were not stellar models for functional relationships (I don't know *anyone* who had perfect parents). We worked hard to move from the dark side to the delightful side of marriage. We don't take each other for granted and we don't coast, even though positive momentum makes it easier to stay on track.

My friends don't buy it. They still clamor for another Victor. (*Hey, what am I, chopped liver?*) When I tell Victor about his fan club, he smiles and winks at me. Then I smile. We remember how rough it was in the early days of our marriage. We like it better as it is now. And nothing, not even an airline ticket, can change our commitment to and affection for each other.

14

The color of money is red

Not long ago, I plopped myself down at my desk to do some 'ciphering about how much ADD has cost me over the past thirty-five years.

I didn't count the emotional cost (which has been substantial) or the cost to my relationships (also significant). I added up only the actual, honest-to-goodness, bought-and-paid-for receipts that were directly attributable to my ADD. I'm not an accounting whiz kid, but conservatively, I estimate the total is in the $200,000 range. It's probably more than that, but I had to stop. It was making me dizzy.

Wow. That's a lot of money spent on doctors, psychologists, and counselors (including no-show fees because I forgot the appointments); ADD medication, supplements and alternative treatments; medical bills for broken bones and other urgent care issues; credit card over-limit charges, late fees, and interest; self-help books and classes (some of which I didn't read or attend); missed concerts and plays; duplicates of things I misplaced; duplicates of things I didn't remember I'd already bought; library fines and the cost of replacing missing library books; extra fees for day care when I ran late to pick up the kids; rebate coupons that expired before I could mail them in; gym memberships I didn't use; housekeepers, organizers, coaches, and handymen; movies I rented that I'd already watched; broken eyeglasses, crystal pitchers, and computers; overdraft charges, tax penalties, and interest; body work on my cars after accidents; and a whole lot more.

No question about it: owning an ADD brain is expensive. The costs aren't limited to the results of our procrastination, distraction, or ADD treatment, either. My list didn't include my prefrontal cortex's stupendous ability to ignore the future in favor of Right Now which certainly influences my ability and willingness to save for a rainy day. And I didn't include the results of my biggest ADD nemesis: butterfly shopping, also known as impulsive spending.

If I were a rich ADDiva

If ADD folks had a rich aunt who provided a bottomless, bubbling spring of money, all would be well in ADD land. We are really good at using and spending money—so much so that we might be considered *wunderkinds* at money consumption.

My husband calls me a "world-class shopper," a title I embellish every time I shop for hours online researching minute differences between brands of thermal underwear.

In the bad old days when my children were young and the mall was a good place to take the stroller, I blew our budget out of the water over and over again by succumbing to those tempting displays in department stores. When I realized the error of my ways, I weaned myself away from the mall and butterfly shopping.

Even today, I avoid the mall when possible. But now the mall comes to me, via that cunning little flat screen on my desk: the internet and its many shopping portals. Butterfly shopping has returned and now I need a more stringent anti-shopping strategy.

Ka-ching!
The money
disappears

Sometimes, my spending is less about consumerism than it is about moving forward on my latest brilliant idea. I need raw materials for my brilliant organizing system. I need battery recycling kits to save the planet. I need a desk that fits over my treadmill so I can walk while I work. Those expenditures are important and deeply satisfying—but they still undercut my pledge to spend less and save more.

Truthfully, our wealthy relatives might not stay wealthy for long if they allowed us to indulge our marvelous ideas and amazing good tastes. No matter how much money we have, we seem to spend all of it, a real-time demonstration of the adage, "Money burns a hole in your pocket."

"Stella's" story
(not her real name, but a true story)

I was raised to "save for a rainy day" and to "save more than you spend," but I must have been born into the wrong family. Spending money makes me feel good. Nothing cures a day of depression like some good old retail therapy! New clothes, new shoes, new makeup—heck, it could even be buying new deodorant, and I feel better.

When I turned eighteen, I got my first credit card. Two years later, my "saving" parents paid it off for me. After I got married, I got another credit card. Pretty soon, it was maxed out—so I cut up the card. I thought I had conquered my spending.

A few years later, I applied for credit cards in my name. Before long, I had six cards (with $5,000 limits) charged up. I was having an affair with money and my husband had no idea, but I was consumed with guilt, so I finally told him.

An acquaintance of mine waited impatiently for her long-overdue divorce settlement to arrive. It was a hefty six-figure amount which was paid to her in a single lump sum. The settlement included her half of the marital house as well as some spousal support that was to last for several years.

The color drained from his face, but he took me in his arms. "We are married, we are a team, and we will get through this together," he said. *"But please—promise this won't happen again."*

It didn't happen again for a long time. And then it did. Two years ago, we used some of our home equity to pay off my credit cards again. When we wrote the check, my sweet husband looked at me with that same look of despair. "Babe, I'm almost sixty years old," he said. *"I can't keep doing this."*

That killed me. As good as it feels to spend money, I have to reconcile myself to the fact that I cannot control money. It controls me. It's like an addiction. I handed over my credit cards to my husband for safekeeping so I can't spend impulsively.

Now I know that my ADD is part of the reason I got into debt. That's not an excuse, but it is an explanation. And I am learning that I am not an untrustworthy slimeball. I am a woman with ADD who is discovering ways to control it rather than allowing it to control me.

She could have made a down payment on another house, but within eight months, she had spent every dime of the settlement, and was living in subsidized housing. To this day she's not sure where the money went or what she was thinking when she went a little "retail crazy."

My suspicion is that she had lived in a tight financial box since her separation and her pent-up demand for spending simply overwhelmed her. When she was married, her spending was offset by her husband's salary. Now that she was single, she hadn't developed the necessary fiscal restraint to apportion her windfall over several years. And with an ADD brain, she'll probably continue to have trouble curbing her impulse to buy.

We love "new" things that engage our brain and make life interesting. There should be a string of those annoying, blinking, red lights around that fact: *DANGER, DANGER, Ms. ADDiva! Financial ruin ahead!*

Disciplined folks, who spend moderately and balance their checkbooks every time they spend three or four cents, sometimes shake their finger disapprovingly at our spendthrift ways. But they don't understand that spending money tickles our ADD brains where they need it most: right in the dopamine (Mr.

Dope A. Mean) receptors. In some circles, Dope is known as the "pleasure molecule," which I consider an apt and fitting tribute.

Whee! Slide down the reward cascade!

To prod our dopamine into action, the human brain plays a neurological game of Mousetrap (remember how much fun it was to crank the handle and watch the Rube Goldberg-like sequence trap the little mouse under the plastic cage?). Scientists call it the "reward cascade." One little neurotransmitter turns the crank, which stimulates another one, which inhibits a third one, which wakes up a fourth one—and so on and so on until we catch our old friend Mr. Mean (dopamine) in the cage.

For normal folks, the reward cascade maintains a sense of wellbeing and keeps stress down to a roar. But in ADD brains, there is a piece missing from the game, so the reward cascade is short-circuited and we miss our dopamine fix. Our brains cry "uncle" and urge us to choose a new route to happiness. We scramble to find something, anything, that will bring the pleasure molecule back into the picture.

From a chemical point of view, the good news is that there are several excellent supplements readily available to tease dopamine out of hiding. The bad news is that the

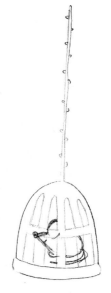

Catching dopamine in the mousetrap

supplements include alcohol, cocaine, heroin, marijuana, cigarettes, and glucose (fondly known as "carbs"). These bad boys kick butt in the dopamine department, but they have some nasty side effects.

We want more and more of them to keep our dopamine levels high, which explains our predisposition toward addiction. Add the push-me-pull-you effects of insulin and blood sugar, and it's easy to see why so many ADD women spend time on the carbohydrate roller coaster. Our dopamine receptors are hungry!

Although they may not meet strict criteria for addiction, behaviors like shopping and sex satisfy our craving for dopamine, too. Spending money can be a nearly orgasmic experience for many ADD women (and many ADD men, for that matter). There have been real, honest-to-goodness studies that prove window shopping doesn't complete the reward cascade; we need to plunk down money in exchange for products or services to get the dopamine rush.

Scientists also know that when we use our charge cards to buy things, we don't feel the true "cost" until the monthly bill arrives. There is a mental disconnect between a string of numbers imprinted on a piece of plastic and the limits of our disposable income.

One of my early clients used her credit card to buy everything she needed for her young family: groceries, toys, restaurants, clothing, gas, rent. She made regular monthly payments to the credit card company, so she couldn't understand why her balances were going up instead of down. She'd never used a budget. When we sorted out the bills and paychecks, we found that she was spending $1,200 a month more than the family income. The twist to this story is that my client was an assistant professor of mathematics at a private university. ADD trumped her graduate school expertise.

Her experience points out a knotty problem for ADD folks: money management. Asking someone with an ADD brain to manage money is like asking a fish to ride the proverbial bicycle; it's difficult, if not darned near impossible.

Money, management, and ADD

From a distance, I admire budgets. They are neat and orderly. They have nice little rows of numbers lined up next to each other like those pretty Victorian houses in San Francisco. Up close and personal, however, budgets are a bit, shall we say, rigid. Those unyielding numbers demand accuracy, and worse—accountability. They sneer at us when we try to pay attention and then stick out a foot to trip us when we don't. I have respect, but not admiration, for the budgets that live at my house.

Yet budgets are the foundation of managing money. ADD adults, whether they like it or not (usually not), must have at least a rudimentary tracking system for money-in and money-out. Creating a budget really isn't so bad; adding up expenses and plotting them out on a monthly chart is pretty basic stuff. The challenge comes when we of the ADD persuasion try to stay within the confines of our budgets.

I compare staying on a budget to maintaining a newly-organized desk. We are neat and conscientious at the outset, but as time passes, our resolve weakens (and our attention wanders). We end up with a messy desk and/or a budget that is out of balance. This is not simply the result of impulsive spending or overindulgence. Mastering money requires repeated, regular, and diligent focus, and none of those things are on the Top Ten Hit Parade for ADD adults.

Dealing with money also requires math skills. Admittedly, these skills aren't as complex as calculus. But talk to anyone who has misplaced a single decimal point in an account ledger and you'll learn the power of math-induced frustration. And remember that ADD folks are prone to dyslexia (intermingling letters) or dyscalculia (numbers that jump into the wrong column), which also makes balancing our checkbooks infinitely more fun.

Are ADDivas allergic to math?

By the time we've reached midlife, most of us have reached an uneasy truce with money; we have some way of dealing with it so the bills get paid and the electricity stays on (most of the time). We have unpleasant memories of threatening phone calls from bill collectors, so we try to keep our account balances in the black instead of bright red. Some of us even have a little savings tucked away for a rainy day (but even more of us have already borrowed it to pay for an emergency). Only a few of us have invested enough to live the rest of our lives in comfort.

Yesterday, today, and tomorrow

I'm always sure there is enough time to put money away for retirement. Tomorrow. Or maybe the day after that. But one day soon, I will be ready to retire and there will be no money, no IRA, no SEP, no golden parachute, nothing. Which means that I probably won't be retiring.

Right now, that's not such a terrible thought. I am still healthy and vibrant. But what happens in fifteen or twenty years, if I break a hip or have a serious illness? I will need to survive financially even when I'm not working. That's quite worrisome; I might be out of money when I am at my most vulnerable.

Many years ago, I started a retirement account. I promised I'd make deposits every year, watch my balance grow, and feel proud that I was finally acting like a grown-up. I made exactly two deposits. Instead of growing, my balance was thwarted by a sinking economy. I have the same amount of money I started with (which is a relief) but it's not enough for security.

I wish I could rely on rich relatives to take care of me in my old age, but sadly, I have none. It's up to me to stabilize my financial future, a quite unfriendly proposition for my ADD brain. To step up to the financial planning plate requires three distinct, yet critical, components: 1) a goal to which I can aspire; 2) a prefrontal cortex with a good plan; and 3) money.

Setting a financial goal is easy: I want to live the rest of my life with ease and flow while I take care of my health, my family, and my community. Inviting Ms. Prefrontal Cortex to the party is more troublesome. She is still taking those extended coffee breaks and does not like to be interrupted. But I need my "planning department" in action to move this plan forward. A bit of caffeine or some ADD exercise might entice her back to work. Or I might find assistance from an ADD-aware financial planner who can help keep me on track.

Another coffee break?

Then we come to the toughest component: cold hard cash. For me, that means earning money from my job. And employment is a tricky proposition for many ADD women. Not only do we find gender inequity in the workplace, we also have brain inequity. And that dramatically impacts our annual and lifetime incomes. The time has come to stare down the Darth Vader of finances for ADD: work.

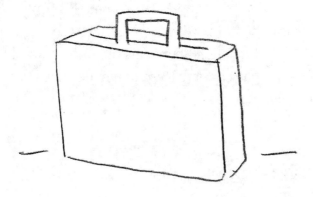

15

ADDiva goes to work

always thought I'd earn my first million by the time I turned thirty, but I didn't.

I was sure I'd be mayor of a medium-sized city by the time I was forty, but I wasn't.

I expected Oprah to invite me to be on her show by the time I hit fifty—but she hasn't called yet.

So, is my professional life a failure? Not by anyone's standards but mine. I am painfully aware that I have never been as successful as I thought I could—or should—be. I still lament the fact that I took the GRE (Graduate Record Exam), the GMAT (Graduate Management Admissions Test), and the LSAT (Law School Admissions Test) but didn't go to grad school, even with a scholarship to study law.

I wish I would have taken that job as a TV reporter at a network station back in 1985; I might have been an anchor for CBS by now (but only if I'd had my first facelift by age thirty-five, I was reliably informed).

The progression of my career is chock full of "if only" and "I should have" notes crammed into one of those ceramic jars labeled "Regrets." I know I'm not alone in my despair.

We midlife ADD women share a profound sense of failure and underachievement, no matter how many letters are after our names, how many awards we win, or how many people we supervise. We are more likely to be underemployed; some of us are barely hanging on to minimum-wage jobs, even though we know we're smarter than our boss.

We change jobs more frequently, find it difficult to move into management (or to stay there if we are promoted), or get fired for repeated infractions (being late, forgetting direct instructions, speaking our minds to the boss, etc.). We have more unplanned pregnancies (think impulsivity) so we may have "lost our place in line" during our childbearing years.

Many of us had difficulty in school—dense textbooks do not engage our brains—so we didn't finish high school or college or trade school, which thwarts our employability and our paychecks. Even those of us with impressive credentials tend to earn less than our non-ADD counterparts; we can't stay on track to get tenure or win the sales contest trip to Bermuda. By the time we reach our forties and fifties, our career picture has tilted askew. It's time to take stock of our lives.

When I looked at my aging resume, I could read the truth between those neatly-typed lines: I'd been working at full throttle for years with precious little to show for it.

Finish high school, finish college, get a job

That sequence was drilled into my head as a child, an adolescent, and a young woman. So that's what I did. Sounds simple. It wasn't. Like every other project in my life, I had a little trouble finishing.

My attention span for high school lasted three years. Unfortunately, I went to a four-year school. Thank goodness I was accepted into an experimental Independent Study program for my senior year. No required classes, just research, term papers, and end-of-year exams. Uh-oh. ADD procrastination ahead.

Though I graduated with honors, it was by the skin of my teeth. At the last minute, my chemistry teacher changed one question on one test, which changed my grade from a B+ to an A-, which pushed my GPA up to a 4.0. It was the lowest grade point average of anyone sitting on the Honors Stage.

I was accepted at several Ivy League colleges, but I turned them down, dreading the possibility that my unpredictable academic performance might take a nosedive. Instead, I opted for a land grant school that offered me a place in their Honors Program. No freshman requirements! No attendance requirements! No structure! Not good for ADD!

By the middle of my sophomore year, my GPA had fallen below 3.5 and I was kicked out of the Honors Program. By the end of my junior year, I dropped out of college altogether to get married. It was an embarrassingly un-feminist choice, prompted less by my desire to settle down than by my avoidance of life and career decisions.

As a child, my career aspirations had been appropriately unrealistic: I decided to become a famous ballerina, unaware that passion was no substitute for a lithe, athletic body (I despised wearing "Chubbies"). I later decided to become a famous doctor. I had the grades and the ambition to go to medical school, but I was secretly afraid that I wouldn't be able to stick with school for eight more years.

I was in awe of television journalists; I thought they must be the smartest people on earth since they had the inside track on important events and people. Network television anchors Barbara Walters and Jessica Savitch were my journalistic icons, but I was cautioned that only beauty queens were hired for TV; the rest of us Plain Janes would be relegated to writing obituaries at a newspaper.

So I crafted a more pragmatic, yet equally ambitious, plan: major in advertising, then move to New York City to follow in the footsteps of Mary Wells, the first woman on Madison Avenue to establish her own advertising agency. Her firm was renowned for its creativity; it won Clio awards for the "plop-plop, fizz-fizz" Alka Seltzer commercials, for instance. *Creativity*—now that was something my ADD brain could grab with gusto.

The alternate route

I launched my advertising career by writing copy for radio commercials at a local AM-FM station. I was happiest when I was allowed to thrash around creative ideas to develop a catchy slogan or a sixty-second spot. But creativity was only part of the job description. My work hours were set in stone. I had to deliver products on deadline. I had to attend staff meetings and deal with surly co-workers. In other words, I rammed directly into dull, routine job duties which dampened my enthusiasm for work.

An unenthused ADDiva is an unmotivated ADDiva. The grass always looked greener at another job. Since my then-husband was climbing the corporate ladder, we moved often, which gave me an excuse to quit my current, boring job and find a new, more exciting, soon-to-be-boring one.

Intuitively, I sought ADD-friendly jobs with high stimulation and a minimum of desk time. I spent most of my workday in the field as a reporter for radio, TV, and newspaper. It was a near-perfect occupation; news is unpredictable, so no two days were alike. I never knew when a sniper would hole up in a downtown building or I'd be called on to board the Sky 11 helicopter for a live shot 200 miles away.

But news cycles could also be deadly dull. Writing stories about school buses and the first day of school got old the second time around. Celebrity interviews weren't nearly as thrilling as they sounded, and sitting through traffic court and school board meetings were painful for my ADD brain, not to mention my body. My colleague joked that the two of us had bunions on our butts from all those meetings.

My performance reviews were good, but there was usually a footnote about my tardiness or rushing through projects at the last minute. The most serious problem I encountered occurred when I worked in sales, a popular field for ADD folks.

In those days, I was selling radio advertising. I won almost every new sales contest, but I wasn't good at follow-up (also typical for ADD). I made the fatal mistake of neglecting a key client, and I got fired. *Fired*. I can scarcely type that word. I was only unemployed for twenty-four hours; I had plenty of supporters who were outraged at the station's decision. But fired? *Me?* I was crushed.

I vowed to hunker down, nose to the grindstone. My next few jobs were uneventful, but they sapped my energy. I was simply not cut out for regular hours and hum-drum tedium.

Once bitten

If you aren't independently wealthy, there are only two alternatives to being an employee: starve to death or work for yourself. After Victor and I were married, I had a small degree of financial security, so with his encouragement ("I'm happy at my job, I want you to be happy at yours") I launched my own writing and marketing company, Exclusive Writes, Inc.

Many ADD women test the waters of being our own bosses. It looks like a win-win situation: escape from Cubicle Nation, 100 percent flex time, no supervision. But ADD can undermine the best-laid business plan. (*Business plan? Do other entrepreneurs have business plans? I never got around to finishing mine.*)

My firm was well-respected in the business community and it grew quickly. Soon, I expanded our range of services, hired employees, and moved into office space. It was heady stuff, handing out business cards with the title "president" printed under my name.

Behind the business-like facade, though, I was up to my ADD eyeballs in responsibilities that were more linear than I had ever imagined. Employee reviews, payroll taxes, client meetings, crisis management; they added up to seventy-hour weeks and a cloud of anxiety that haunted me. No one but me held the vision for the company. No one but me needed to bring in revenue to pay the bills. No one but me stared at the ceiling in the middle of the night hoping beyond hope that we'd sent the final proof to the printer and not the draft.

Despite my determination to stay on top of our clients' needs, I was stretched so thin that I repeated my radio station nightmare: I let projects fall through the cracks and our biggest client began to shop for a new agency. This time, I saved the day; with a strong recommitment to follow-through, our client returned to the fold and the company rebounded.

My "overcoming the obstacles" story was so compelling that the local chamber of commerce named me the Micro Business Person of the Year ("micro" referred to size of my company, not my stature!). I accepted the award proudly, cameras snapping. Outwardly, I was riding the crest of success—but behind the closed doors of my corner office, I knew the truth: I didn't deserve this honor.

My ADD inattention had caused the problem in my business in the first place. It wasn't right to reward me for fixing a problem that was my own fault. I felt like an entre-preneurial fraud at many levels.

Only my employees knew about my serious time-management problems. They often arrived at the office in the morning to find me working at my desk wearing yesterday's clothes. (I used to say that when my employees went home, my workday began.)

My ADD brain had trouble with prioritization, which is pre-cisely the reason I had allowed those client projects to slip away. I managed our finances on the back of yellow Post-it Notes (which worked better for me than complicated spread sheets). And I wasn't making a salary that befitted the CEO of a supposedly successful company.

I lived in fear that someone would peek behind the curtain and notice that the vibrant Business Person of the Year was a business woman who was dog-paddling as fast as she could to keep her head above water.

Terms of employment

I've talked to a lot of ADD business women, some wildly suc-cessful, some less so. Almost to a person, they report that they, too, have felt like a fraud at some point in their careers. They say they hide their ADD-ish traits from clients and employees and bosses. They walk around with a sense of unease that they will be exposed and their ADD brains deemed unworthy. Yet our ADD traits can be our best friends at work.

Our bosses *need* our creative problem-solving skills. Our clients *need* our brilliant ideas (we've got a million of 'em!). Our employees *need* our enthusiasm and resilience (we keep bouncing back, no matter what). The world *needs* our contributions. The trick is to find or create a work environment that favors instead of censors our ADD-ish ways.

That can mean either choosing a field that fits us or working for a boss who teases out the best in us. It certainly means taking the time to find the right company and the right position. Does this mean we should all find ADD-friendly jobs? You bet. But where are they? And even more importantly, what *are* ADD-friendly jobs?

The ADD recipe for professional success

ADD manifests in so many different ways, it's impossible to isolate a specific set of occupations for all ADD women. The right choice depends on knowing our ADD strengths and playing to them.

High stimulation works well for many ADD women. Creativity works well for others. Lots of structure is important for some of us, but more freedom is better for others. Some of us work best with noise and chaos, while others work best in the quiet. Whatever helps our brains engage and focus (think interesting tasks) is the best employment fit for the ADD adult.

There are successful ADD emergency room physicians who thrive on the never-a-dull-moment crises. There are ADD landscape designers who can happily spend hours plotting trees and shrubs. There are creative ADD chefs who love the loud energy of a kitchen at mealtime, and there are ADD librarians who appreciate the hush of study carrels and stacks of silent books.

We are paramedics and writers, engineers and actors, clergy women and construction workers. A successful career depends on understanding and accommodating our own unique "brand" of ADD.

My ADD is a bit loosey-goosey, so I needed a workplace that afforded me the chance to move around regularly. I needed a career with both creativity and stimulation. I also needed the structure of deadlines so I could finish the projects I started.

In retrospect, I can see that I set up exactly the right work environment for my ADD when I founded Exclusive Writes. Our projects changed constantly; there was never a dull moment.

After being an entrepreneur for several years, I found out that most small businesses (managed by ADDivas or not) run aground on their own decisions. The difference for Exclusive Writes was that I recovered, pulled back from the dark abyss of failure. So I wasn't a fraud after all. I *did* deserve that chamber of commerce award!

To tell or not to tell

I suspect that my ADD honesty played a role in my entrepreneurial success. I always played it straight; my no bull-hockey integrity was the direct result of my "get to the bottom line" ADD impatience. I simply didn't have the time or energy to wade through a web of business politics; I was in business to serve my clients. Period.

That earth-shattering honesty is seen in many ADD women. It can get us into trouble if we are indiscriminately honest at work. I'm talking here about telling the boss about our ADD.

When we finally get (or believe) that we truly own an ADD brain, it's tempting to tell everyone we know so that they, too, can finally understand what makes us tick. Why we're late. Why we are messy. Why we forget to take out the trash on Wednesday nights.

In a perfect world, sharing our story would be a welcome release. But in today's less-than-perfect world, being open about mental health issues raises suspicion, possibly among some of the people who control your professional life. They believe that if something is off-kilter in our brains, we must be crazy. Or they dismiss our ADD diagnosis as trivial or imaginary. There are still people in the world who don't believe that ADD exists, and you never know when you're going to run into one of them—even at work.

DON'T Tell

While I am a strong proponent of coming clean about ADD, in the current job climate, I think it's wise to keep that information out of your workplace if at all possible. It's easy to sidestep the ADD conversation when you are performing well on the job. But if your ADD is causing problems at work—if you are on the cusp of losing your job, for instance—it seems counterintuitive to sit on information about ADD.

The harsh truth is that your employer, even if he or she likes you as a person, doesn't really care about your ADD. They just want the job done. If you can't finish the project on time, you are expendable. If you can't focus, you aren't carrying your weight. If you aren't doing your job, you are out of a job. It's that simple.

Before there is an outcry of "foul play," let me say that ADD is indeed considered a true disability and is singled out as part of the Americans with Disabilities Act (ADA). That means we should be able to request and get accommodations at work that will help us do our jobs. We don't ask for much: a little extra time on projects, written instructions, or a quiet room to prep for a meeting. But even seemingly minor accommodations have been shot down in court when ADD employees have sued their employers to get assistance.

For now, the best way to balance our ADD needs with the requirements of our job is to use non-ADD language to set up accommodations for ourselves. Instead of dragging out the big guns ("My ADD makes me inattentive to details, so I need you to itemize the steps on every project.") we can soft pedal the words to achieve the same result ("I know how important this project is to the company, so would it be possible to get a copy of the original outline, so I can make our department look good?").

In the future, my expectation is that we'll be able to be forthright about our ADD at work. My vision is that employers will not only accept our ADD brains, they will welcome our thinking style. They may even have a recruiter for ADD employees. The conversation with Human Resources might sound something like this:

"Help! We just lost our best ADD employee; the competition lured her away for double the salary. We are desperate. I don't care what you have to pay, get us another ADD person as soon as possible!"

Until then, we ADDivas can dig deeper into our ADD; knowledge is power. And we can craft a career that tickles our ADD fancy. Now, if you'll excuse me, I hear the phone ringing. It might be Oprah.

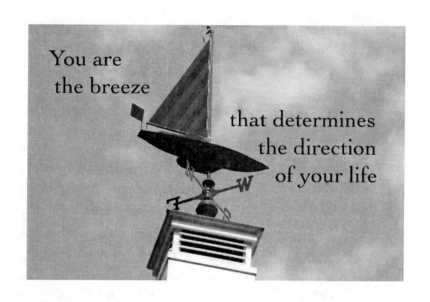

You are
the breeze

that determines
the direction
of your life

A-D-Diva

(ay-dee-DEE-va)

1. a woman with ADD-ish tendencies. *see also*: inquisitive, creative, **spontaneous**, resilient, **passionate**, authentic, **sensitive**, determined, **honest**, optimistic, **forthright**, generous, **innovative**, loyal, **engaging**, compassionate.

16

Viva! ADDiva!

few years ago, my husband and I went out for dinner and movie. I can't tell you where we ate or the name of the movie; but halfway through the film, as the young hero was consoling his angst-ridden girlfriend, these words tumbled from the screen into my life:

"Why are you trying to fit in when you were born to stand out?"

Victor immediately turned to me. "That's you!" he whispered excitedly. "I keep telling you that you were born to stand out, so stop trying to be like everybody else!"

Something stirred deep within me, a familiar ache that longed for release. For years, I had dimmed my light, stepping aside to allow others with more confidence, more focus, and more direction to set guideposts for me. The Monitor had done such a good job of maintaining my public persona that I rarely discarded it, even during private moments. I had resisted piercing its tight armor to let the Real Linda out to play, fearing that once released, she would never again be forced into hiding.

And yet, all I had ever wanted was to dance my own special dance, to be truly, fully me. It was one of the most grievous tragedies of my existence that the world refused admittance to the Real Linda.

From early childhood, I had understood that there was something special about me—not "different" in a negative way, but in a wonderful and exceptional way. I could never quite find the key to unlock her before the ravages of social decorum beset me and the Monitor took over my internal discipline.

I admired women who had the courage to color outside the lines and who were eventually respected for their lack of conformity, like barefoot ballet dancer Isadora Duncan and actress Katherine Hepburn. I, too, wanted to unleash the full range of my creativity and passion. I wanted to be applauded for being me.

As I mulled over the line from the movie and Victor's invitation, I realized that to shed the security of my public persona, I needed to upgrade my status in my own mind from "deficient" to "whole and complete." I needed an infusion of positive strokes and high self-esteem. I needed to love myself, including my ADD brain.

Is it normal to be normal?

When we talk about ADD, it's usually in the context of "something wrong." That, by definition, means that there is a standard by which we categorize "something right"—in other words, behavior that is judged "normal."

But consider this: if 95 percent of all adults owned ADD brains, ADD would be considered "normal." Because the numbers are reversed—experts estimate that only 5 percent of the adult population has ADD, and an even smaller percentage is officially diagnosed—then it is our brains that get squished into the jar labeled "Abby Normal," like the one in the movie *Young Frankenstein*.

Yet, in *Young Frankenstein*, even the monster with the Abby Normal brain learns to sing and dance. It proves that when you put a monster in a tuxedo and shove him onstage, he can pass in polite society as "normal" or possibly even "exceptional."

I could don the equivalent of the monster's tuxedo so I, too, could "pass" for normal. But that defeats the point of being exactly Who I Am. There's nothing especially attractive about falling in line with the rest of the lemmings.

"Normal" is what we see around us. I have talked to many ADD women who grew up believing that ADD was the standard; they thought their ADD families were normal until told otherwise by the experts.

We have an unhealthy intolerance for "differences" in our culture: thin or fat, wheelchair or legs, black or white, gay or straight, linear or non-linear. They are all relative. Even within this unforgiving culture, we can make a choice to accept our ADD brains—because for us, they *are* "normal."

It's really not such a big deal that we show up late to lunch. We aren't the slug of the universe when we miss a deadline. Life doesn't end when we procrastinate on finishing a paper (or a book). There is more to life than toeing a line in the sand that was drawn by someone else, someone who used a straight edge and a pointer.

Reframing ADD

When I stepped back a few inches from ADD literature, I looked at the clinical language with new respect and healthy skepticism. In only a few decades, researchers and scientists have raised Attention Deficit Disorder from a moral issue to a legitimate medical condition. Treatment is now covered by insurance companies. With the exception of a few outliers, most people accept ADD as a real disorder, even if they see it as an issue that pertains only to children (we know better!).

Reframing ADD

In the process of elevating ADD's stature in the scientific community, the very language used by professionals elicits hopelessness and sadness. When they toss around gloomy terms like "impairment," "maladjustment," and "poor self-regulation," it's difficult to be upbeat about our ADD prognosis.

Words are powerful. The way we describe ourselves reflects how we view ourselves. When we steep in negative associations, it takes a toll on our psyche and self esteem. If I think of myself as "defective" or "deficient," I am unlikely to "stand out" in a way that makes me proud. In fact, that kind of thinking pushes me further in the secret ADD closet.

So I made a quite conscious decision to reframe my ADD in a more positive light. I focused on my strengths instead of my deficits. I replaced the word "impulsive" with "spontaneous." Rather than "distracted," I am now "curious" or "fascinated." When I "hyperfocus" on a project or task, perhaps I am actually "determined" or "tenacious."

I wrote a definition of an ADD woman (an ADDiva) that includes words like "unique," "resilient," "innovative," "passionate," "flexible," and "inquisitive." I could add "intuitive," "sensitive," "courageous," "honest," and "resourceful" to the list. Not a negative connotation among them.

Surely it's not this simple; sugar-coating ADD doesn't cure it. But there may be more validity to the power of positivity than a light dusting of powdered sugar.

The Power of Positivity

Martin Seligman, Ph.D., founder of the Positive Psychology Center at the University of Pennsylvania, has popularized the concept of "learned optimism." Dr. Seligman's work is far more scientific than Pollyanna's cheerful admonition to "think

happy thoughts." He and his colleagues have conducted gold standard research to show the benefits of optimism.

They found that, when people are optimistic, they live longer, have fewer mental and physical health problems, and enjoy better relationships. Women who focus on their strengths have fewer heart attacks than the control group. That's pretty impressive—but changing our attitude toward ADD doesn't change the fact that our brains are still misfiring their neurotransmitters. Or does it?

Only a few years ago, researchers were certain that our brains contained a static number of cells and that a brain would normally shrink with age. Current research shows that human brains have "plasticity"—they grow new cells when stimulated, and our neural pathways can be altered. This is not to suggest that we can "think ourselves" out of ADD. But it is encouraging news, especially when coupled with the outcomes of optimism research.

Please sir, I'd like some more

There's an esoteric slogan that floats around the self-help atmosphere: "What you focus on expands." If I need a new refrigerator, suddenly the world is full of refrigerator ads. They're in the Sunday paper, on the internet, on billboards.

Of course, the ads were always there, but when I focused on them, the number "expanded."

The same is true with ADD descriptors. If I focus on the problems with ADD, I will find even more problems, and they will expand in my life. If I focus on what is right about ADD—or more accurately, about myself—I will find more things that work for me instead of against me.

I'll admit, I am a born skeptic. I was raised in a family of pessimists. The glass wasn't half full or half empty; there wasn't a drop in the glass! Most of my professional career was spent as a working journalist. News isn't "hard news" unless it's bad news, so I was trained to ask questions that would uncover a scandal or catch the politician in a lie. On the personal side, far too many people had made snide remarks behind my back. My instinct had been to recoil and retaliate with equally negative energy.

So I was more than a little cynical about looking for the "up side" of ADD. As part of my emergence from the ADD closet, however, I was willing to give it a try.

Long ago, I read a forgettable book with a forgettable character who made a quite memorable statement: "Act as if." Act as if you are happy even if you are depressed. Act as if people are good even if they have treated you badly. Act as if problems will be solved easily, even if they are as stubborn as baked-on barbeque sauce. The expectation is that if you pretend life is getting better, it will actually *get* better.

This wasn't a new idea; it paralleled the familiar "fake it 'til you make it" slogan, which offended my integrity. I believed that, if I felt depressed, then I should act depressed. But acting depressed was getting me nowhere fast. I decided to try faking it; "acting as if" life was positive. I had nothing to lose.

Luckily, I was in a coaching training program that emphasized what was right and perfect about our clients, our coaching, and especially ourselves. This airy-fairy, everything-is-wonderful attitude was so utterly foreign to me that I had a hard time fighting off the Monitor, who screamed that this was silly drivel. But I persevered.

As I made my foray into "positivity territory," I learned to reinterpret negative events so I could find something positive about them. I quelled my instinct to criticize and use sarcasm in favor of listening with an open heart.

I not only discarded the burdensome clinical language of ADD, I put a positive spin on my own ADD. I took ownership of my creativity instead of sneering at it as something to quash. I honored my sensitivities as extra antennae for collecting more data from the world around me. I noticed how spontaneity added vigor and vitality to my life.

A funny thing happened on my way to dispel the idea that positive thinking was a delusion. My life took an honest-to-goodness upward turn. When I focused on positivity, it *did* generate more positivity; positivity was truly expanding!

Roots of realism; wings of hope

There is a chasm in the ADD professional community. On one side are the science folks who require hard evidence so that they can document the serious repercussions of ADD—more driving accidents, higher substance abuse rate, more divorces and failed relationships, less education, and lower income. On the other side are folks like me who look for the positive aspects of ADD.

Just because I choose to focus on what's right about my life, it doesn't mean I don't understand (and live with) the consequences of ADD. Of course it's frustrating to still lose my car keys, even with keyfinders that have bells and whistles. You bet I am still embarrassed when I miss my hair appointment because I was hyperfocused on the internet. I fall victim to shame when other people notice that I am wearing my shirt wrong side out. ADD is often a problem.

But as I did with Erica, the professional organizer, now I laugh gently at my mistakes. I apologize when necessary (but never to doorknobs) and fix what I can. And then I go on my ADD-ish way with a lilt in my step and a smile on my face.

Fitting in is overrated; I am ready to stand out in all my ADD-ish magnificence.

17

The Journey

It was already a terrible, no good, super bad day for my company—and I hadn't even set foot in my office yet. My office manager had called me at home, her voice anxious.

"We've been robbed!" she said. "The police are here. They need you to file a report."

Robbed? Our security system had been breached and burglars had been prowling around our offices? I was speechless. Owning my own company had never been a cakewalk, but I'd never imagined (nor planned for) this kind of snafu.

The burglars had apparently started their spree in the real estate company on the first floor and then made their way upstairs. By the time they'd reached our offices, they had worked up an appetite. The thieves polished off the leftover food in our refrigerator, hung out in our break room, and then attempted to steal the copier. They rolled it down the hall, but it wouldn't fit in the elevator—so just for kicks, they poured an entire can of icky-sticky orange Hi-C all over the top, where it seeped into the fragile electronic panels. Goodbye, copier. Goodbye, security. Goodbye, Exclusive Writes.

Although I didn't know it as I filled out the insurance forms, the robbery marked the beginning of the end of my firm. My adrenaline system was fried from the rollercoaster excitement of meeting advertising deadlines, recruiting new clients, training employees and managing finances.

I had worked with Cindy, my business coach, for a couple of years, but instead of boosting my performance, I felt that we were backsliding. In my private moments, I had fantasized about closing the company and walking away. But I couldn't bring myself to do it; my clients depended on me, my employees were loyal and capable, and my reputation was still intact.

I had set up the perfect corporation for my hyperactive, creative ADD—yet I wasn't happy. I cried every day on the way to work, then sat in the parking lot to dry my tears and bravely paste on my "boss face" before I entered the building. This was no way to live.

Finally, I closed my eyes and took the plunge. By the end of December, I had laid off the last of my employees, given notice on my lease, sold most of my office equipment, and moved the rest back home. I had done it at last: taken care of myself instead of everyone else.

Desperately seeking answers

As we reach "that certain age," not only do our periods "pause," but our life circumstances evolve, too. Children move on and out. Grandchildren arrive for some of us. Retirement looms large.

We are restless, ready for answers to life's Big Questions: Who am I? What direction shall I take now? How can I spend the rest of my life with passion and purpose?

For those of us diagnosed with ADD at midlife, there are multiple levels of awareness that prick our consciousness. We grieve the wasted time we spent coping with our unidentified ADD, but we also see a glimmer of hope. Perhaps, now that we have come to grips with this slightly weird brain of ours, we can begin anew—and have a rebirth of sorts.

There is a world of difference between us and younger women who discover their ADD brains in their twenties. They have decades of youthful opportunity ahead of them. We don't. The choices we make now, while better informed and cognizant of our ADD, carry more weight because we are acutely aware of our own mortality.

> "The choices we make now, while better informed and cognizant of our ADD, carry more weight because we are acutely aware of our own mortality."

We see it reflected in our own parents, who may have passed on or who need our care. We see it in our mirrors, in the gray roots that peek from under our hair color and the smile lines that crinkle around our eyes. Life is short. We want to make the most of it using the new knowledge about our brains to best advantage.

Now that I had shed the responsibilities of my company, I wanted to spread my arms wider to include my ADD in the next iteration of my life. But I was heading for fifty, fast. I didn't have a chance for many more "do overs" in my life. I found myself in an quandry: "What do I want to be when I grow up?"

Starting from scratch

In February, a friend of mine invited me to her graduation from a self-improvement program. I had been to these gatherings; they were merely a way to gain new members. I had a migraine and had two other commitments that night, but I felt an obligation to her, so I showed up ... late, of course.

During the evening, the rah-rah facilitator led several exercises, one of which was interactive. I dreaded it. My head hurt and I didn't want to talk to anyone. I was on the verge of slipping out the back door, but I got caught up in the exercise anyway. The instructions were to project yourself five years into the future, living your ideal life, and then tell other people in the room about your good fortune.

Even though it was the dead of winter, I had been working on our yard to prepare for my husband's fiftieth birthday party. It was to be an outdoor celebration, and a very special one, since my husband has cystic fibrosis and had never expected to make it to age fifty. That hard, physical labor and reconnecting with the Earth had cleansed my anxiety like nothing else. So I knew I wanted to do something that involved gardens and plants.

I started by introducing myself: "Hi, it's so good to see you. Yes, my nursery is on forty acres outside of town. Things are going so well, it's amazing." Every time I told this imaginary mini-story, I grew more uncomfortable. Thankfully, the exercise ended and we were allowed to return to our seats. At the front of the room, as the facilitator gushed about the value of visualization, I started a conversation with myself.

"You don't want a garden center. You don't want to take care of other people's plants. You don't want to do retail. You don't want more employees!"

My mind was quiet for a minute, and then it asked: "Well … what do you want, Linda?"

"Oh, I'll think about that later," I answered in my best Scarlett O'Hara voice. But my mind was relentless.

"You always say that," it nagged. "What do you want?"

Another moment of quiet.
"Well, I want a place to write. I want something to do with women and spirituality and gardens," I told myself slowly.

Then the heavens opened and spilled the words directly into my head: "A women's spiritual garden retreat."
Of course! How had I not seen it before?

I walked away from the graduation ceremony a changed woman. I didn't sign up for the course; I didn't need it. Now it

was up to me to execute this vision while holding hands with my ADD. I was confident and excited.

From here to there

I set about visualizing my dream. I imagined how it would look, smell, and feel. I pictured how the rooms would be decorated and I saw the secret gardens and communal kitchen. I told a few people about my dream; they were wildly enthusiastic.

At Victor's birthday party, I mentioned my plans to a friend, who also happened to be married to Victor's boss. She stood close to me and asked in rapid succession: "How much land do you want? Where do you want it? What are you going to do with it?"

I pushed her back a little. *What was up?*

"We have 100 acres of raw land," she said. "Talk to my husband about it."

Her husband was easy-going about the land. He even mentioned a lease of something reasonable, like $1 a year! I panicked slightly. This was happening too fast. I had put an intention out into the universe and it was responding "Yes!"

A couple of months later, we toured the property. On the way, the owner told us that the Corps of Engineers had bought some of his land for conservation, which meant it would never be developed, which was good. The remainder of the property now totaled …. forty acres, the exact acreage I had mentioned during the graduation exercise. My stomach took flight. Perhaps this retreat center would become a reality!

Although this tract of land was wonderful, wooded, and beautiful, there were a few drawbacks. The house had burned down; the property was landlocked and would require an easement for access. I had no money stashed away for construction or permits. So it wasn't the ideal site for what was soon to be known as GardenSpirit Retreat Center. The 117 acres owned by a dear friend of mine just across the Virginia state line wasn't a good fit, either.

GardenSpirit took shape, literally, in my back yard; we bought the house behind us. I decorated the interior in soft pastels and soft linens. I planted daffodils and crepe myrtle and painted the tree house purple. I created a sixty-foot outdoor labyrinth and meditation paths. My dreams had come true.

Co-creators of the dream

More precisely, I had co-created my dream, with help from my husband and the Universe/God/Goddess, a force that is more powerful than I had ever imagined. Along the way, I trained as a spiritual retreat facilitator with Neale Donald Walsch, author of a series of books about conversations with God; I became a spiritual life coach and a facilitator for Full Presence Communication through Speaking Circles.

In 2005, I facilitated my first women's transformational retreat. The women—who called themselves the "Pelicans" after the name of the retreat beach house—are still in close contact, sharing their lives with each other. I continue to facilitate retreats, my true calling. It is an unending joy to witness the blossoming of other women as they, too, discover their own wisdom and purpose.

Trust yourself

This, then, was my True North, the right and proper direction for my life. It had taken all those previous experiences—the highs and the lows—to arrive at this place. It had taken my ADD brain. It had taken willingness to sit quietly and listen to that "small still voice." It had taken faith.

If I had skipped past just one of those milestones, regardless of how unpleasant they had been in the moment, I never would have arrived here at this place of serenity and deep satisfaction, the place that is me.

The journey we choose for ourselves can be changed at any moment. We have all we need to embrace a new beginning, to start fresh, and to look at the world through new eyes.

No matter whether you are late or impulsive, whether you daydream or talk circles around your friends, there is still hope for you. If I can do it, starting at age fifty, you can do it, too. Make this life your own. Claim it all. You are the gift the world needs now.

trust your path

even when
you can't see
what's ahead

18

Born to be extraordinary

Back in my pre-ADD awareness days, I held a mental image of my life as a dense jungle, completely shaded from the sun. I slashed at the vines and tried to cut paths through the thick undergrowth, but I could make no progress. I was constantly lost.

Then, one miraculous day, I found a smooth tree that arched gently toward the top of the vines. I climbed carefully and slowly. Suddenly, I broke through the undergrowth to see crystal blue skies and to feel the sun on my face.

Even though I was just barely above that tangled jungle floor, I had a completely new perspective on life. I could see where I had come from and, more importantly, I could see where I was going. I could see the possibilities—and they were limitless. For the first time in my life, I didn't look to the experts for answers. I knew deeply that the wisdom I needed for my journey was already within me. I could finally trust myself.

It's hard to believe I once thought that I was so damaged and so different that I couldn't be "fixed." Now I know I don't have to be "fixed" to be the perfect person to guide my life. I only have to love myself for being exactly Who I Really Am.

That's enough.
For me. For you. For all of us, ADD or no.

So, yes, we were born with ADD brains. That means we were born to be extraordinary in every beautiful sense of the word. We are ADDivas, every one. From this moment forward, our lives are forever intertwined. We are bound together by our ADD, by our beautiful brains, by our amazing and clever personalities, and by our innermost wisdom.

No matter what has happened to you in the past, no matter how much pain you have endured or how deeply the arrows have penetrated, you, too, can find a smooth tree at the bottom of the tangled jungle floor and begin to climb toward the sun.

Here, give me your hand and we will climb together.

Give me your
hand and
we will
climb together.

Viva! ADDiva

Epilogue

(or how to write a book in just four years)

I t was 114 degrees in Scottsdale, Arizona the summer of 2007. Four hundred of us were staying at a luxury hotel to train with the legendary Jack Canfield.

I had followed his work for years and knew that the week would culminate in a "future" party. Each of us would arrive in character— the character of ourselves as we would be when we had achieved our goals, a version of the graduation ceremony that had brought me the idea of GardenSpirit.

I had decided this would be the week I would launch the ADDiva Network. My "future" character would arrive at the party promoting her latest book about the Network. But there was a small glitch in my party plans: I had no idea what this imaginary book would be, how it would look, what it would say, or to whom.

Two days before the party, I emailed my graphic designer in Los Angeles and asked her to design a book cover. I impulsively dreamed up a temporary title: *Confessions of an ADDiva; Life in the Non-Linear Lane.* That title would do for the party, anyway.

I printed the cover at Kinko's, wrapped it around Dr. Tom Brown's latest book about ADD, and made my way to the festivities. When I showed the book to Canfield, he grinned and told me he loved the title. He "got it" because his writing partner for the *Chicken Soup for the Soul* books had ADD.

It has taken four years, but I have made *Confessions* the permanent title of the book you hold in your hands or are reading on screen. I "acted as if" and created my new reality to match my dreams.

It hasn't been easy. My husband went through a scary medical crisis that he barely survived. GardenSpirit was closed down by local zoning officials until I jumped through a lot of ADD unfriendly hoops.

I still have ADD; I procrastinated a lot, even when I hired a book coach to push me through the writer's block. I set a goal of finishing the book in January 2010 so it could be sold during a conference in May. It wasn't done. I set another goal of finishing the book by the end of the year. *Didn't happen.*

In January 2011, I knew it was time. I set another goal: to finish writing the book and publish it by my birthday, April 29. Keep in mind that I had chapter outlines and bits and pieces of drafts scattered here and there, but nothing really completed except the first chapter, which had been revised eighty-three times.

I unearthed an old pledge I had written to myself, about midway through the process of writing the book. In part, it said, "If I could only get away from here, to write at the beach, I could finish the book."

I don't think I really believed I would ever finish the book. But there was a nagging voice—which sounded a lot like my assistant, Janie—who told me again and again that *Confessions* needed to be out in the world. So I made a gigantic leap.

I found an oceanfront beach house on the coast of North Carolina and I booked it for a month. *A month!* I had never done anything like that before. I took the dogs with me, along with a bunch of paper, my computer, and a printer—and I went to work. It was miserably cold at Emerald Isle. The first few days, we were fogged in; I couldn't even see the ocean. It was a perfect metaphor for my book. I couldn't see my way through the writing, either.

Gradually, I buckled down, spreading file folders—one for each chapter—the entire length of the fourteen-foot, varnished kitchen table. I created a temporary desk from an array of adjustable-height tables that had a view of Bogue Inlet Pier. And I began to write.

I wrote while the dolphins pranced in the shallow surf. I wrote at midnight. I wrote at dawn. I wrote until my computer died and the company sent a replacement to the beach house (bless you, Apple!). I wrote until I slipped on the slick, hardwood floors and broke my elbow. I wrote with my arm wrapped and my pain meds on board. I wrote and slept. Wrote and wept. Wrote and wondered if I would ever find my way to my favorite four-letter word: D O N E.

When the dogs proved to be too much of a distraction, I sent them home early. Then I extended my stay by two weeks. I wasn't DONE. I took walks on the chilly beach, including one at 4 a.m. when thick fog had settled along the coastline. It was magical. I met a retired school teacher from Michigan who sang Jimmy Buffet songs to the ocean. I dried laundry in the winter sun on the decks. I warmed myself by the fireplace in the evening. And I still wasn't DONE.

I came home. I wrote a bit, then stalled. I wrote a bit more, then stalled again. Time was running out. But the best inspiration is always a deadline and the goal was still my birthday. I doubt that anyone else believed I could meet that deadline except my husband. He has seen my determination at full throttle and knows that I will plow my way through ice floes to succeed.

If you are reading this, then I did it. If I am the only one reading it, then I did not. But I suspect I did. Even with my ADD.

Ironic, isn't it? I wrote about ADD and my own ADD quite nearly prevented me from delivering the book. I can say with certainty that this book was a labor of love. When I wrote, I was thinking of you, hoping that my "confessions" would soothe you, comfort you, console you, inspire you, and offer you hope.

But the book was also my personal triumph—a triumph that lays down the gauntlet for you to deliver your own labor of love, your own dream. Remember, all we have is time. It's time you created a reality you love. Get the help you need. Believe in yourself. Then live into your own passionate possibilities.

in moments of uncertainty
we are guided by the markers
left by those who have walked this path

Lagniappe goodies

"Lagniappe" (pronounced "lan-yap, like a yapping dog) is a New Orleans term that means 'just a little extra'—like getting an extra 10 minutes on your massage or a 13th donut. So go online to download these juicy ADDiva lagniappe goodies!

Bonus chapter

I promised not to include tips and tricks in this book, but if you visit the *Confessions* website you can download your ADDiva bonus chapter with all kinds of information about:

- How to find ADHD doctors & psychologists
- Medication and alternatives to meds
- Coaches & professional organizers
- AD/HD gadgets (only my favorites)
- Nutrition and supplements
- My favorite tips and tricks
- Grocery shopping list for your refrigerator
- Join the ADDiva Network at no cost!

Download it right here:
http:www.addiva.net/confessions
The secret password is: **EXTRA**

Acknowledgments

I always compare the acknowledgments page to a thank you speech at the Oscars—mentioning everyone would take all night. So I'll write an abbreviated, ADDiva-friendly version so you might actually read it!

Of course, kudos must go to my book coach, Judith Kolberg, who waited (somewhat impatiently) for me to get DONE with *Confessions*. She offered great advice (some of which I actually used), spent a long weekend with me at the beach house while I tore apart Chapter 4 again and again and most of all, she never gave up on me. That touches my heart more than I can express.

Pamela Guerrieri of Proofed to Perfection, who bravely waded through my manuscript at the last minute, did a thorough yet thoughtful job of editing.

My medical mentor, Tracy Ware. M.D. saved me from embarrassing mistakes about the neurology of ADD and has been an inspiration from the day I met her. Thank you for stepping bravely into the ADD arena!

A deep bow also goes to Dr. Jerry Lithman, the heretofore unnamed psychiatrist in "This is my brain on ADD" who has worked with me and my ADD for years. And to the therapist before him whose name I have temporarily forgotten (I must have ADD; my memory is fading), a humble round of applause.

This book would never have reached completion without the enthusiastic and loving support of my long-time assistant and partner in ADDiva crime, Janie Wilson. Never let it be said that you have not lived up to your potential; you are an amazing woman whom I am proud to call my friend and colleague!

And to Janine Futch, who has been with me even longer than Janie although in a different capacity; you are a treasure! A follow-through kind of gal is what every ADDiva needs in her life. You have been here through thick and thin and I appreciate you deeply.

There aren't words to describe my affection and gratitude to Erica Edelman, my stalwart professional organizer and dear friend who didn't walk out on me or my piles.

The 560-plus members of the Triangle AD/HD support group I facilitate have been a constant source of information and encouragement, too. Co-facilitator and friend Mary Fulton has never flagged in her support and camaraderie. And I especially want to thank my clients, my marvelous clients, who astonish me every day with their courage and determination to live full lives, even in the non-linear lane.

I have been touched and inspired by the work of such ADD luminaries as Pat Quinn, Sari Solden, Kathleen Nadeau and Terry Matlen. Many thanks to Ari Tuckman, Nancy Ratey, Stephanie Sarkis, and Kim Kensington. And of course to other icons in AD/HD land: Ned Hallowell, John Ratey, Tom Brown, Russ Ramsay and many more. A special thanks to my own AD/HD coach Jen Koretsky.

I know it seems a little far fetched, but I want to publicly acknowledge the owners of the beach house that birthed *Confessions of an ADDiva*, Craige and Lisa from California as well as the long-term rental agent from Bluewater & Associates at Emerald Isle who ran interference on my behalf. Those six weeks marked the turning point in my confidence and my chapters.

Finally, I can't say enough about the support of my darling husband, Victor. You've met him through these pages and probably understand how much I rely on him. He boosts my spirits when I deflate; he believes in me far more than I believe in myself and he cherishes me in a way I never dreamed possible. He is my heart. Well, to be frank, the dogs hold a piece of my heart. Little Milli, Boomer and senior Cosmo share our home, our food and sometimes our bed. To all the home folks, I say thank you and good night.

Uh, I guess I ran over my five minutes on stage. Drat. I went overboard again.

April 29, 2011

About us

Linda Roggli, PCC, is a professional certified coach and the founder of the ADDiva Network, a whimsical and supportive connection for midlife women with ADD-ish tendencies.

She organizes and moderates a 565-member AD/HD adult support group that meets twice monthly in central NC. She has conducted educational webinars for the ADDiva Network since 2007 and for ADDA since 2006. She is a popular presenter at national AD/HD conferences and is a contributor to and guest blogger for *ADDitude* magazine.

In 2006, Linda established GardenSpirit, a women's garden retreat center, on eight acres in suburban Durham, NC which includes a 60-foot-outdoor labyrinth, purple tree house and meditation paths.

She trained as a spiritual life coach before stepping into AD/HD coaching in 2005; she now holds certification from the International Coach Federation and Coach for Life.

She is the author of *Durham: Doorway to Discovery* (1995) and *Angie's Choice* (2005). In her spare time, she teaches organic gardening and plays with her three adorable Shelties and one fabulous husband who often co-facilitates her AD/HD couples' retreats.

Visit her at www.addiva.net.

Wendy Lynn Sefcik is an illustrator/designer/author, owner of Broken Box Designs, LLC (a custom illustration & design studio). She's addicted to artsy things and obsessed with color!

She is a Summa Cum Laude honor graduate of The University of Akron with a Bachelors Degree in Fine & Applied Arts. Wendy lives in Northeastern, Ohio with her family.

For more information visit www.BrokenBoxDesigns.com.